KEEPING TRACK OF WHAT YOU SPEND:

The Librarian's Guide to Simple Bookkeeping

KEEPING TRACK OF WHAT YOU SPEND:
The Librarian's Guide to Simple Bookkeeping

by Brian Alley and Jennifer Cargill

ORYX PRESS
1982

The rare Arabian Oryx is believed to have inspired the myth of the unicorn. This desert antelope became virtually extinct in the early 1960s. At that time several groups of international conservationists arranged to have 9 animals sent to the Phoenix Zoo to be the nucleus of a captive breeding herd. Today the Oryx population is nearing 300 and herds have been returned to reserves in Israel, Jordan, and Oman.

Published by The Oryx Press
2214 N. Central at Encanto
Phoenix, AZ 85004

Published simultaneously in Canada

Printed and Bound in the United States of America

Library of Congress Cataloging in Publication Data

Alley, Brian
  Keeping track of what you spend.

  Bibliography: p.
  Includes index.
   1. Library finance.   2. Library administration.
I. Cargill, Jennifer S.   II. Title.
Z683.A44   025.1'1   81-11289
 ISBN 0-912700-79-3   AACR2

Contents

Acknowledgments

The authors are especially grateful to Robert Huebschman, Internal Auditor at Miami University, for his sound advice and helpful suggestions. He is our example of a friendly, helpful auditor. Special thanks goes to Judy Sims, Account Clerk, Miami University Libraries, for her assistance, and to Jacalyn Kearns and Teresa Kolb for their typing expertise. We also thank our friends and colleagues at several institutions: L. Ronald Frommeyer and staff, University of Cincinnati Central Library; John S. Wallach and staff, Dayton-Montgomery County Public Library; James R. Hunt, R. D. Stonestreet and staff, Public Library of Cincinnati and Hamilton County; the Minneapolis Public Library staff; Thomas L. Reitz, Seminole Community College Library; Marion T. Reid, Louisiana State University Library; and Maurice C. Libbey, Eastern Illinois University Library. Their suggestions, information, and assistance were invaluable.

Introduction

Keeping Track of What You Spend was conceived when we realized how little had been written on internal financial systems for libraries. Budget planning and allocation formulas have been covered regularly in the literature, but the mechanics of managing the funds once the money has been allocated are often neglected. From libraries surveyed in preparation for this book, we found mixed results. Many libraries had good internal bookkeeping systems and had devised procedures and forms over the years to fit their particular needs. Far too many other libraries, however, did not have systems that precisely monitored the use of funds. Even simple recordkeeping seemed beyond their grasp. These libraries spent until they were broke, or thought they were, and then worried about the consequences.

Many librarians are resigned to a career of inept fiscal management, and those who see the problems are often faced with unconcerned colleagues. Many librarians are not aware of accepted business practices and do not feel obliged to adopt them. Others consider the business aspects of library management to be unprofessional. Perhaps for these reasons, many librarians appear to have a cavalier attitude toward money, budgets, and the mechanics of budget control and expenditure. Fear of the unknown, lack of business acumen, an impatience with details, or a combination of all 3 may have contributed to this avoidance of matters involving money. Whatever the causes, the result has been a weakness in some libraries where fiscal matters are concerned.

WHO NEEDS IT?

Most libraries are part of a larger organization such as an academic institution, a public library system, or a regional system. The degree of financial independence ranges from complete autonomy to none at all. Some libraries can commit their funds and even write checks to pay invoices. Others can commit funds and approve invoices for payment but the parent organization reserves the authority to control expenditures by issuing the checks. Finally, in some organizations, the library may select what is to be ordered but all commitments and expenditures of funds are processed in a central office. Even libraries that do not actually handle the mechanics of committing and expending funds have found it advantageous to keep track of their financial transactions. This enables them to commit all funds fully, to ensure expenditure of the entire allocation in the time allowed, and to provide safeguards against overspending.

WHAT IT IS

Keeping Track of What You Spend, then, is an overview of practical methods for monitoring the committing and expending of funds, techniques for surviving an auditor's visit, and methods for operating an internal financial system day-to-day within a library ranging in size from very small to fairly large. With a collection of suggestions, proven routines, and sample forms, we hope to provide both alternatives to trial and error fiscal management and a sense of confidence in dealing with one of the two most important and often neglected aspects of the librarian's daily routine: people and money. The sample procedures and forms included may be readily adapted to suit the individual library.

WHAT YOU CAN DO WITH IT

Libraries may require an internal system to follow expenditures for books and periodicals or an internal system may be necessary to monitor supplies, equipment, and personnel budgets as well. These internal systems often serve as a check on the accounting system maintained by the parent organization, whose reports may be weeks or months behind the spending reality of the library. Internal controls also aid in budget projections during a period of inflation. For example, monitoring the unit costs of books and periodicals may seem unnecessary to a central accounting office, but it is a useful budgetary tool which librarians will find increasingly necessary in coping with inflation. In the final analysis, administrators who lack sufficient data on budget expenditures are unable to make sound planning decisions. Acquisitions librarians and subject specialists are unable to function effectively without fiscal records and reports.

These are the areas or people within the library who will benefit from an internal accounting system which provides needed support and information:

- Supply and equipment purchaser.
- Payroll personnel.
- Order/Acquisitions librarian(s).
- Collection development personnel/book selectors/subject bibliographers.
- Circulation staff.
- Shipping and receiving personnel.
- Library administration.

Often, when a new aspect of fiscal management is imposed on a library or a librarian, there is a need for ideas such as how to set up routines, where to start, what forms to use, and what pitfalls to avoid. At worst, the novice will attempt to follow a trial and error route. At best, a colleague who has a reputation for sound management will be consulted. Few librarians possess accounting skills, yet they must develop bookkeeping systems or must supervise such systems. In some small libraries, the librarians are required to do the bookkeeping rather than relying on other personnel.

AUTOMATED VS. MANUAL SYSTEMS

The widespread use of automated accounting systems is one answer for many libraries. Yet even those libraries fortunate enough to afford an online, automated system must have a grasp of the basics of internal accounting before they become involved with automation. It is vital for a library to know what it wants and how it wants it presented before accepting any automated system. Unless based upon a firm understanding of the library's own financial routines, the transition to an automated system will be a matter of guesswork,

creating problems that could have been avoided with better planning and preparation. Readers anticipating an automated future can adapt the procedures in this book and use the forms included as a basis for their preparation for the computer age.

Many other libraries will find that institutional policies and/or budgetary restraints prohibit the use of any automated system, ensuring the need for a reliable manual system. For many libraries, an online system will never be economical. Small libraries, in particular, which emphasize service to their clientele will need a simple, straightforward manual system to monitor the use of funds and to guarantee the expenditure of every dollar while freeing the staff to provide public services.

Accordingly, we have provided procedures and examples that do not require special accounting skills. They are basic to money management in the same way that your checkbook satisfies your need to monitor your own personal expenditures. We advise you to establish a system or revise an existing system to meet the fiscal control needs of the library without spending time and effort on expensive, superfluous recordkeeping.

WHAT IS THE END PRODUCT?

In some large organizations, library purchases may be processed by the purchasing and accounting department of the parent organization. In these situations, the library provides the basic order and receipt information for the central authority to perform its functions. The result is that the library has virtually no control over its budgetary expenditures. In other organizations, the library makes the initial purchase commitments but must funnel the necessary documents through a central purchasing and accounting office. Finally, in still other organizations, the library may initiate purchases and prepare the fiscal documents for payment after receipt of the goods or services. Whether your library is in one of these 3 situations or in yet another variation, you may soon find that an internal accounting system is needed to assist in determining the amount of money not encumbered and expended: the free balance.

The library may receive periodic reports from the centralized financial offices or, as in the case of some public libraries, bank statements, but these reports may be days, weeks, or months behind what is actually occurring on a daily basis within the library. A library may, therefore, need an internal bookkeeping system to assist the purchasing agents within the library. This in-house system may be part of an automated system that offers fund accounting. However, most libraries still—and for the immediate future—must rely upon a system that is at least in part manual. Even after an automated system has been installed, many libraries, especially the smaller ones, will need some form of manual system to fill in the missing details which have been neglected by the automated system and to accommodate any special accounting or reporting requirements that have not been programmed into the larger system.

A given library may have the authority to make purchase commitments primarily in the area of books and periodicals. That library may also have some authority to contract for certain services, supplies, and equipment within general guidelines established by the governing authority. If the central administration is willing to allow the library to enter into purchasing obligations, it is incumbent upon the library administrators to provide adequate safeguards, in the form of procedures, to keep the library purchasing routines simple, up-to-date, and within budget limits. It is vital that the organization devise ways and means of ascertaining exact and current fund balances to ensure: (1) that there are adequate funds available for the purpose at hand, and (2) that as orders are generated, those funds are formally encumbered, and thus held, until they will be needed for payment.

The only record the parent organization has of the library expenditures may be a computer printout of checks drawn on various library accounts as payments to vendors. This printout may not be available until weeks after the actual invoice is paid; thus the information is of no value in determining accurate account balances. This computer-generated report may also fail to indicate internal, unofficial encumbrances—that is, commitments to purchase—thus creating even more questions about the status of actual balances. Knowing what has been actually paid is an important element in managing any budget, but that information arrives after the fact: when that payment transaction has already been completed.

Certainly of equal importance is the process of encumbering purchase commitments. These encumbrances allow you to reserve funds at the time you generate your purchase order so you'll be able to pay when the invoice arrives. So much of a library's total business is transacted in terms of thousands of individual book and periodical requests that unless the amounts on each purchase order are accurately recorded in your internal bookkeeping system at the time of the commitments, it will be impossible for you to know whether or not you will have sufficient funds to pay the invoices when they eventually arrive. If you encumber

the $29.95 price of a book you order today, you will be sure you will actually have the $29.95, minus any discount and plus any shipping charges, available to pay the invoice when it arrives 3 weeks hence.

THE IN-HOUSE SYSTEM

Within the library, an accounting system providing current records of encumbrances and expenditures, even though an unofficial system, often provides the necessary controls to prevent the library from overspending or, equally disastrous, underspending. The presence of such a system provides an accurate reflection of daily library spending activity.

A simple mechanism for controlling expenditures includes: a current recordkeeping system so that you can make regular commitments and expenditures with complete confidence and assurance, and which allows your internal purchasing to proceed with a minimum of concern for whether or not there are sufficient funds in a given account to cover specific expenditures. The system should allow the library to close the fiscal year with all accounts balanced and reconciled with the central administration records. You must also make certain to build in a series of audit trails which will allow an auditor to trace a library purchase through the order routine back to the original request. The actual internal accounting system a library selects depends upon the amount of autonomy given to the library by the parent organization.

Figure 1 presents examples of 3 library fiscal systems, each of which can profit from a simple internal accounting system. Library A simply funnels purchase information to a central office which in turn initiates the purchase and expends funds, leaving the library with an incomplete record of the fiscal process. Library B initiates the purchase order, then funnels all fiscal documentation to another office. Library B has a clearer picture of the fiscal process than does Library A, but still needs a way to ensure that its portion of the overall ordering and payment process is being adequately controlled. An internal recordkeeping function is an integral part of Library C's purchasing system. Library C initiates all purchase orders and requests that payment be made by another office; thus, it has accurate records of all financial transactions—assuming that it reviews the reports of checks which have been mailed.

In many colleges and universities and public library systems, library-materials purchasing often consitutes the largest block of single-item ordering. If the

xii Keeping Track of What You Spend

central purchasing department were to issue all library purchase orders, the result would be a general slow-down in ordering and an increase in personnel for the purchasing department. Because many of these libraries have the authority to issue purchase orders in the name of the institution, it is incumbent upon them to create and maintain accounting records which provide complete documentation for every library fiscal transaction.

FIGURE 1. Three types of library fiscal systems.

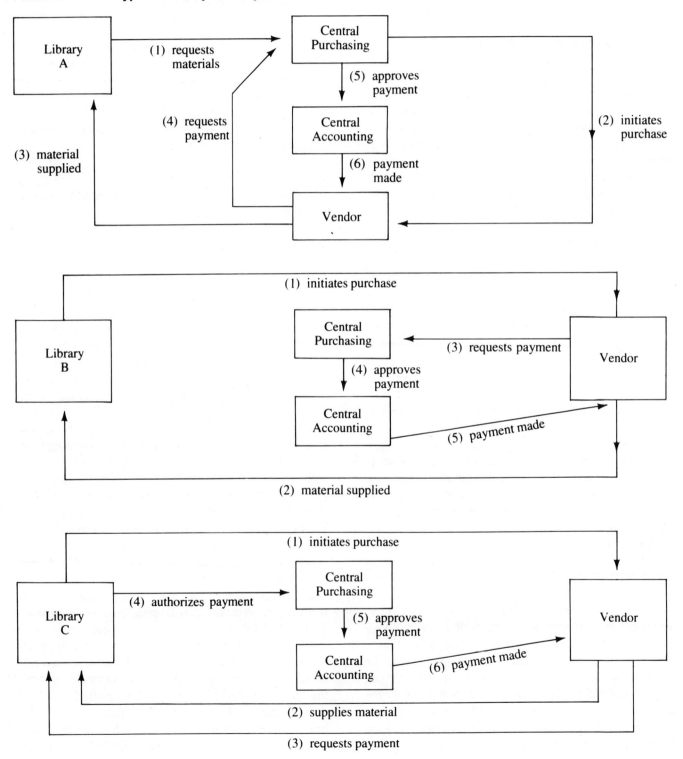

Chapter 1.
The Basic Ingredients: Staff and Materials

STAFF

Once the decision to produce an internal accounting system has been made, the next step is to determine who will supervise the activity and who will actually carry out the routine clerical functions. The person responsible for supervision should be the same individual who is accountable for purchasing and bookkeeping activities, including preparing and submitting regular budget reports. Practical experience in the day-to-day business activities of the library is a major requirement for the supervisor. Many directors and head librarians have the authority to make purchases and approve payments; however, they are usually too far removed from the actual business activities and may have no familiarity with the standard accounting and purchasing practices.

Large public libraries may already have an internal accounting system and the organization to go with it. This could include a business manager or clerk treasurer who, as the senior library fiscal officer, oversees the entire business operation, including all the accounting functions. Thus, small to medium-size public libraries and junior and four-year colleges have the greatest need for simple, accurate accounting systems. Few of these libraries have staff with accounting and bookkeeping qualifications, while the size of the library's personnel budget usually precludes hiring a specialist to do the work. The bookkeeping system that is adopted should be relatively easy to learn and simple to operate with existing staff.

Staff and Skills Requirements

A bookkeeping system cannot be devised and implemented overnight. Systems must be revised and modified over the years, through sometimes painful development. In the early stages, the ability and skill of the account clerk and the supervisor will have a great deal to do with the degree of success achieved. Later on, as additional proven techniques and procedures are built into a manual operation, the individual ability of the personnel becomes less critical to the operation.

In a smaller library, a librarian handles the actual recordkeeping, while a larger organization provides a clerical assistant to perform the same routines. There is no doubt that accounting expertise and skill are vital ingredients for this position. Workload may vary from a few records to a mountain of detailed accounting work to be processed daily. A person who has already acquired accounting skills has an obvious advantage in this position. Speed and accuracy are particularly necessary if one person does all the posting, balancing, and file maintenance needed to keep encumbrances up-to-date. As the job grows, additional assistance may be needed.

Since libraries tend to fill many business management positions with librarians rather than other professionals with specialized training, you must rely upon the business-oriented librarian who has practical experience in handling the purchasing and accounting activities. By placing the responsibility for accounting with the person who does the buying and approves the expenditures, the supervision will be in the hands of someone already familiar with library business activities.

Job Descriptions

The following examples present typical job descriptions for these clerical positions, within the structure of the state civil service, a public library, and an academic library. Portions of and terms from these descriptions may be adapted as appropriate in designing particular jobs.

EXAMPLE I. State Civil Service Job Descriptions

Account Clerk Supervisor

Job Duties

Supervises accounting section within department or institution; interviews applicants; trains new employees.

Audits, analyzes, & supervises preparation of invoices, purchase orders, time reports, inventory, etc.

Answers inquiries & requests according to established procedures; assists lower level account clerks with more complex problems.

Collects, analyzes, & prepares financial reports of complex nature.

Performs related clerical duties (e.g., types correspondence & forms; operates posting machine.)

Major Worker Characteristics

Knowledge of (1) bookkeeping, (2) supervision, (3) office practices & procedures, ability to (4) understand bookkeeping procedures & apply principles to solve practical problems, (5) calculate fractions, decimals & percentages, (6) gather, collate, & classify information according to established method, (7) establish friendly atmosphere as supervisor of work unit.

Knowledge of 1, 3; ability to 4, 5, 6.

Knowledge of 1, 3, (8) public relations; ability to 4, 5, (9) handle sensitive telephone & face-to-face inquiries & contacts with public & government officials.

Knowledge of 1, 3, (10) public accounting; ability to 4, 5, 6, 9.

Knowledge of 1, 3; skill in (11) typing; ability to 5, (12) copy records precisely without error, (13) work alone.

Account Clerk I

Job Duties

Posts various types of accounting transactions to ledgers, journals, or cash books; makes necessary mathematical computations for posting & maintaining records.

Audits, codes, & processes simple accounting transactions (e.g., invoices, receipts, vouchers).

Files cards, invoices, & vouchers; types & proofreads correspondence, statements, & forms; orders & distributes office supplies; answers routine inquiries by telephone.

Compiles & types variety of financial reports (e.g., weekly & annual reports on cash, budget, accounts receivable, accounts payable).

Assists in checking purchase orders, payrolls, time sheets, time cards, vendor checks, budgets, & other such records & documents.

Major Worker Characteristics

Knowledge of (1) bookkeeping, (2) office practices & procedures; skill in (3) typing, (4) operation of adding machine or calculator; ability to (5) understand bookkeeping procedures, (6) read, copy, & record figures, (7) add, subtract, multiply, & divide whole numbers.

Knowledge of 1, 2, (8) government structure & process; skill in 4; ability to 7, (9) deal with problems involving several variables in familiar context, (10) copy records precisely without error, (11) code items from one symbolic form to another, (12) gather, collate, & classify information according to established method.

Knowledge of 1, 2; skill in 3; ability to 5, 9, (13) carry out detailed but simple written or oral instructions; (14) complete routine forms.

Knowledge of 1, 2; skill in 3, 4; ability to 5, 12.

Knowledge of 1, 2; skill in 4; ability to 7.

EXAMPLE II. Public Library Job Description

Account Clerk Supervisor

General Responsibilities

Under general supervision to do supervisory and accounting work of more than ordinary difficulty and complexity in the keeping of financial and other records; and to do related work as required.

Typical Duties

1. Assists in the development and installation of forms, procedures, records, and reports of financial, statistical, or other informational nature; supervises others in the processing of such data; prepares summary records and reports and audits same for accuracy and completeness; balances accounts and prepares trial balances; prepares ledger and journal entries; maintains accounting records of various types; audits and verifies invoices and claims; maintains purchase orders, requisitions, and other files; audits payrolls; checks special assessments; checks assessment rolls; and audits assessments for improvements.

2. Computes costs including distributions of labor, equipment rentals, materials, and overhead according to funds, projects, divisions, and departments; prepares cost statements and statistical reports; maintains materials controls; administers cost accounting controls; supervises subordinate employees engaged in bookkeeping, accounting, and audition; prepares budget; maintains personnel records.

Minimum Qualifications

1. TRAINING AND KNOWLEDGE REQUIRED FOR JOB APPLICATION: Considerable knowledge of principles, practices, and procedures of accounting, bookkeeping, or auditing; considerable knowledge of office methods and procedures and the use of standard office equipment; ability to supervise the work of subordinate employees; ability to meet and deal with others tactfully and effectively.

2. KNOWLEDGE AND ABILITY NECESSARY FOR FULL JOB PERFORMANCE: Thorough knowledge of principles, practices, and procedures of accounting, or auditing; thorough knowledge of office methods and procedures and the use of office equipment; considerable knowledge of the accounts and other records used in the area assigned; ability to keep complex and difficult records and to make detailed reports and statements; ability to supervise the work of subordinate employees; ability to meet and deal with others tactfully and effectively; and ability to make and check arithmetic computations.

Account Clerk I

General Responsibilities

Under immediate supervision, to do routine accounting work of ordinary difficulty and complexity; and to do related work as required.

Typical Duties

1. Journalizes routine accounts; posts accounts to ledgers; makes simple trial balances, posts and proofs bills in control for ledger accounts; assists in taking final balance; prepares statements; posts to perpetual inventory records; operates adding machines and calculators.

2. Files reports and records; answers phones; may make physical inventories; performs related duties as required.

Minimum Qualifications

1. TRAINING AND KNOWLEDGE NECESSARY FOR JOB APPLICATION: Some knowledge of bookkeeping and/or accounting principles and procedures; ability to follow simple oral and written instructions; ability to maintain normal working relationships.

2. KNOWLEDGE AND ABILITY NECESSARY FOR FULL JOB PERFORMANCE: Good knowledge of accounting and/or bookkeeping procedures and principles; ability to follow simple oral and written instructions; ability to maintain normal working relationships; ability to make arithmetic computations quickly and accurately; ability to keep simple accounting records.

Account Clerk II

General Responsibilities

Under supervision, to do accounting work of more than ordinary difficulty and complexity; and to do related work as required.

Typical Duties

1. Posts allotments and charges to ledgers; checks charges for the purpose of controlling expenditures; checks and distributes bills and invoices to the proper expenditure accounts; journalizes accounts; posts to ledger; takes monthly trial balances; codes and approves invoices for payment; codes tickets and/or time cards; assists in periodic audits of fees and deposits collected by various departments; prepares bills; balances with general ledger, appropriation ledger controls, and data processing listings.

EXAMPLE II. Public Library Job Description (continued)

2. Prepares routine reports and statements; assists in annual budget preparation; performs related duties as assigned.

Minimum Qualifications

1. TRAINING AND KNOWLEDGE NECESSARY FOR JOB APPLICATION: Good knowledge of bookkeeping and/or accounting principles and procedures; ability to follow oral and written instructions; ability to maintain normal working relationships.

2. KNOWLEDGE AND ABILITY NECESSARY FOR FULL JOB PERFORMANCE: Considerable knowledge of accounting and/or bookkeeping procedures and principles; good knowledge of modern office methods, practices; ability to execute oral and written instructions; ability to make a variety of arithmetic computations quickly and accurately; ability to maintain normal working relationships.

EXAMPLE III. Academic Job Descriptions

Accountant I

Distinguishing Features or Characteristics of Work

This is professional accounting work of a routine nature. Deviations from established work patterns and precedents are referred to higher authority. A professional level of accounting is indicated by the presence of duties involving the maintenance of various accounting ledgers reflecting a variety of funds, or by the maintenance of controls and balances on a variety of accounting activities, or by the preparation of fiscal statements and reports from a variety of selective sources, or combinations of these activities. In addition to these mechanical aspects of accounting, work also involves the application of professional accounting principles and techniques in the analysis of agency accounting functions to determine the legality and propriety of its fiscal activities and the effectiveness of its accounting systems.

Work is performed in accordance with rules, regulations, and policies of the agency served as set forth in accounting procedures and systems established by higher authority under the provisions of law and administrative directives. Work is usually performed independently within specific accounting areas, subject to review or audit by higher authority. Supervision is received from an agency administrative officer or from an Accountant of higher grade. Supervision may be exercised over subordinate Account Clerks, or over clerical personnel.

Accountant I positions are distinguished from Account Clerk II positions by requirements for the use of professional accounting methods and a professional accounting background as reflected in duties involving a *wide variety* of funds handled, by the presence of balancing operations, by the preparation of fiscal statements and reports requiring professional insight for the selection of data and information to be used, or by *all* of these factors in agency chief accounting officer positions. Complete supervision of Account Clerks II also distinguishes Accountant I positions from Account Clerk II positions.

Accountant II positions are distinguished from Accountant I positions by a lack of complete supervision over an Accountant I or by a lack of responsibilities for performing accounting work of the utmost complexity. In agency chief accounting officer positions, complexity at the second level arises from the multiplicity of accounting transactions, sources of funds, subsidiary records required, variances in types of expenditures, or the restrictions on the use of funds.

Examples of Work

Maintains journals and account ledgers reflecting a sufficient variety of funds to require the use of professional accounting methods and insight.

Maintains purchase order registers and other fiscal records.

Maintains controls, and performs balancing operations on a limited number of accounting activities, or assists in similar operations in larger and more complex accounting systems.

Prepares fiscal statements and reports of a professional nature within specific account limits, or assists in similar activities involving a wider variety of accounting areas.

Prepares fiscal analyses in very limited accounting areas, or assists in such activities in several accounting areas.

Supervises and participates in the preparation of payrolls, preauditing functions and various other clerical-accounting activities.

Qualification Requirements

Graduation from an accredited 4-year college or university with a minimum of 12 semester hours in accounting.

Experience in which accounting or bookkeeping was the primary duty may be substituted for the required college training on a year-to-year basis. The completion of a 9- to 12-month business course that included accounting subjects may be substituted for one year of college training.

MATERIALS FOR A MANUAL SYSTEM

Any manual bookkeeping system should be designed to use materials readily available locally or through a business supply house. The materials should be standard rather than custom-made forms or special order. If, however, you do need custom-made forms of any kind, be sure they can be prepared in the library or locally.

Standard columnar ledger books or columnar analysis pads should be used with a manual system. If your accounting system serves a small library, bound accounting books may suffice. However, you will have more flexibility with analysis sheets you can place in post binders or notebooks. For an active bookkeeping system, the recordkeeping system should be infinitely expandable, something not possible with bound account books.

You will need a set of record books for posting internal encumbrances and expenditures as well as a set for listing payment initiation records or check numbers. Different columnar pages will be needed for the encumbrance/expenditure fund accounts and the payment records.

Forms Design

When the books are being set up for the fiscal year, each page used should be clearly labeled with fiscal year, name and number of fund, allocation amount, and page number. The pages may be prelabeled so that only certain information will be filled in for each fund. Columns should also be labeled to identify the specific activity within each column. To start the year, set up at least one sheet for each fund you monitor. For convenience, the funds should be separated by tabbed pages. Provide an ample supply of prelabeled pages for expansion. By the end of the fiscal year, some large funds with numerous transactions may produce dozens of record pages (see figure 2).

The payment record pages on which vouchers, requisitions, invoices, or checks are listed should also be prelabeled and available for use at the beginning of the fiscal year (see figure 3).

Equipment and Supplies

If many record books are necessary for your manual system, and if these must be stored each day or moved from desk to desk during the course of the day, consider purchasing a cart with several shelves on which these records can be housed (see figure 4).

A combination print and display calculator that can withstand constant use is vital in any internal accounting system. Tapes are useful in reconciling activity, while the display feature makes the ongoing activity easy to follow. Providing a service contract for this piece of equipment is a good idea since it will be used heavily. Even the best calculator is subject to breakdown under constant use; a service contract ensures maximum availability of this equipment. Each person involved in the bookkeeping operation should have a calculator, preferably the print/display variety.

Ink or pencil is acceptable for recording in the accounts. Ink is easier to read, but use of a pencil means neater pages with corrections easily made. If pencil is used, insist on a lead number that is readable without strain.

Additional useful materials include a good typewriter for preparing reports, adequate file space for storing reports and copies of requisitions, and a storage area in which records are placed at the end of each day.

SYSTEM CAPABILITIES

A system with known limitations is better than no system at all. A manual system, whether an entirely handwritten operation or one that uses some special equipment such as posting machines, does have limitations. However, for many libraries the most rudimentary manual system is all that is possible. A library subject to control from another business office may find a manual system all that will be allowed, with any automation efforts being concentrated in the central operation. Unlike those libraries receiving automated fund accounting as an added benefit of automated acquisitions services (such as Brodart's OLAS and Baker & Taylor's LIBRIS), libraries with manual systems need some internal recordkeeping. A manual system is adequate if well designed and maintained, and if its limitations are understood and accepted.

Limitations

When contemplating the establishment of a manual system or when using an existing manual system, keep in mind these limitations:

1. Entering each transaction manually is time-consuming.
2. Errors in calculations or in transferring figures are easily made.

FIGURE 2. A ledger page for encumbering and expending internally within a book fund.

	Date	Vendor	1 Order #	2 Encum.	3 Expend.	4 Total Encum.	5 Total Expend.	6 Unencum. Balance	
		Totals from previous page							
1									1
2									2
3									3
4									4
5									5
6									6
7									7
8									8
9									9
10									10
11									11
12									12
13									13
14									14
15									15
16									16
17									17
18									18
19									19
20									20
21									21
22									22
23									23
24									24
25									25
26									26
27									27
28									28
29									29
30									30
31									31
32									32
33									33
34									34
35									35
36									36
37									37
38									38
		PAGE TOTAL							

BOOKS

Page _____

Year _____

Allocation _____   Fund _____   # _____

FIGURE 3. Official payment records.

		Library Books and Periodicals BOOK Requisitions		Page _____ Year _____					

			1	2	3	4	5	6	7
	Date	Vendor	Req. #	Books	Standing Orders	Approval Plan	Total Expended Books	Total Expended STO	Total Expended Approval
Totals from previous page									

FIGURE 4. A cart for housing records.

3. Success of any manual system is largely dependent upon the people involved. When absences occur or during vacation periods, the reliability of the manual system may suffer.
4. Manual systems are labor intensive and require constant maintenance.
5. The capacity of a manual system is tied directly to staff size and ability. If the staff cannot handle the work load or if many additional funds or functions are added to the system without adequate attention to staff expansion, the total system is bound to suffer.

Advantages

After considering the limitations of manual systems, don't despair. Weigh the advantages of having your own in-house manual system:

1. The bookkeeper needn't wait for access to a keypunch or terminal in order to conduct transactions.
2. Often, certain manual backups are necessary even for automated systems; these manual records must be double-checked against records available via terminal or printout.
3. Unlike automated systems, manual systems are not affected by down time which may occur when programs are changed or systems fail.

4. Manual systems do not require familiarity with data processing, terminals, and networks.
5. System costs for a manual operation are not charged on the basis of time sharing or connect time and may represent only a portion of an employee's duties.
6. Manual systems are as flexible as the people who operate them and can be made to respond quickly to needed changes without costly reprogramming or additional equipment.

A Word of Caution

A manual system will *not* be responsive to library needs if attention is not paid to modifications or if posting and reconciling accounts are not kept current. The bookkeeper and any other personnel working with the system must be constantly alert and ready to make needed changes to keep the system functioning efficiently.

An automated system, on the other hand, may be less responsive than a manual system to local needs. The degree of that responsiveness depends upon many factors, including whether or not a central organizational or governmental accounting system or a commercial turnkey system is used. Most importantly, an automated system that *requires* a manual system for backup or an automated system that is slow or unresponsive is a system you can do without.

Chapter 2.
Putting It All Together: The Mechanics of the System

ACCOUNTS TO MONITOR

The funds a library receives must be allocated to specific accounts, whether the library itself handles its financial matters autonomously or as part of a larger organization. These officially allocated accounts may vary in number from one large allocation to several individual allocations. However the accounts are established, there are certain allocation areas of interest: salaries and wages; books, periodicals, and binding; and the operating expenses. In addition, there may be gift funds, investment accounts, or grants.

The number and type of accounts within a given library budget vary, of course, from library to library, often as a result of the type of library. Some accounts need careful monitoring and others either do not need monitoring at all or do not lend themselves to any internal checks. The most common types of accounts are detailed below.

Payroll. Salary and wage policies and procedures as well as accompanying fringe benefits may be established by law, by the authority governing the library, or by the library organization itself. The major tasks involved with salaries and wages may include recording leaves of absence, sick leave, and vacation. The actual payroll expenditures may be so routine that they require little manipulation from the library staff. The only work to be done by the bookkeeping staff may be routinely processing time sheets or time cards. This recordkeeping may be required for both librarians and support staff, full-time and part-time, as well as for any transient workforce such as student assistants. Even if there are no time sheets or cards for the professional staff, there will probably be some recordkeeping necessary in order to monitor their sick leave and vacation time.

Materials—Books, Periodicals, and Binding. The books, periodicals, and binding accounts will probably constitute a substantial part of the total library allocation. These funds are usually among those requiring the most detailed monitoring. Use of these funds is of great concern to much of the staff as well as to the library clientele. Many subdivisions of these accounts and reports on their use may be required.

Miscellaneous Operating Expenses. The various operating accounts will also be a great concern to the staff as well as to the governing group. These accounts are used for supplies such as paper, pencils, paperclips; purchase and repair of equipment; payment of utilities; travel; petty cash; and numerous other miscellaneous items. Some funds typical of those in the operating accounts would be:

- Travel for staff or interviews.
- Telephone rental and/or toll charges.
- Network or consortium fees or membership dues.
- Automation account including charges for RLIN, WLN, or OCLC; for acquisition or circulation systems.
- Equipment (purchase or leasing).
- Contractual (maintenance contracts on equipment).
- Utilities.
- Supplies—paper, pencils, forms, ribbons, other items too small for equipment fund purchase.
- Interlibrary loan (charges for borrowing).
- Petty cash and change.
- Postage.
- Miscellaneous—items that do not fit other accounts, such as advertisements to fill positions; repairs not

covered by service agreements; TWX/TELEX charges; photocopying; signs; and other incidental expenditures.

Other Accounts: Interest, Grants, Bonds, Monies, and Gifts. A library which can do its own investing, as in the case of some public library systems, will have interest accounts for receipts. This interest may then be distributed on a prorated basis to the other accounts. Libraries that are part of larger organizations may be part of a total investment program. These libraries may not realize immediate benefits from the investment program.

Although government grants were more common in previous years than now, some libraries may still be receiving government support as well as grants from foundations. Public libraries may also have accounts for special capital improvement bond monies. And finally, gift funds may be available to the library in total or in the form of interest from investments. These gift funds often have specific restrictions on their use.

Cost Centers

Various operating accounts may be further dispersed among units where the actual expenditures take place: central libraries, branch libraries, or departments. The amount of allocating necessary depends upon the size of the budget, the number of operating units (buildings or departments) involved, and the requirements of the units. Retaining these operating funds in pool allocations, rather than distributing them among units or fund categories, simplifies recordkeeping but makes it more difficult to determine actual costs of operating the units.

INTERNAL DISTRIBUTION

Internal distribution of funds varies from one library organization to another. Operating funds may be subdivided among agencies so that operational costs can be better identified by area. This breakdown may include apportioning monies for equipment, supplies, and other operation expenses based upon a formula or assigned on an incremental basis. Where there is no formal apportionment, the library administration may require the accounting office to maintain records of fixed expenditures, in order to provide basic cost information relative to the expense of keeping each unit open and available to the public. By adding the additional expenses of salaries and of book and periodical alloca-

tions to these operational costs, it is possible to determine total costs for each unit. In academic situations, however, it may not always be possible to identify all overhead charges.

The accounts most often of concern to the staff and those prone to be divided into subaccounts are the ones used for binding services and the purchase of periodicals and books. These funds are of primary concern to the selection staff who may be under pressure from their library clientele or who may be in competition with library colleagues for a slice of the library budget. The totals of these funds may be used as a measure of the size and value of the system in relation to comparable systems. In public libraries, each branch competes for its portion of the total available funds, often basing its needs on branch circulation figures. In an academic system, representatives from subject areas compete for shares of the monies, basing claims on department size, course loads, collection parity studies, enrollment, accreditation requirements, and even campus political pressures. Let's take each of these budget areas individually and explore ways of dividing them among agencies.

Binding

The binding allocation may be a fund expended on a first-come, first-served basis as periodical or other binding services are needed or it may be broken down among several departments or units. Before any allocations are made or any charges are deducted from the total allocation, the library should first determine the extent of fixed, in-house binding costs. Any costs incurred from the use of laminating machines, spiral and other specialized binding equipment, forms used for binding, pamphlet binders, tapes, and similar supplies should be deducted from the total binding allocation. Traditionally, many of these items may have been considered supplies. However, since they are purchased specifically for binding purposes, they should be charged to the binding allocation.

In some academic institutions, a separate fund may be set aside for binding theses and dissertations. Not only should such a fund be separate and distinct from the main binding budget, but it also should be funded by the organization charged with collecting the fees, such as the graduate school. If, however, it is a part of the library binding fund, the estimated charges for the year should be deducted from the total binding allocation before any further divisions are made.

Ultimately, apportioning allocations may resemble one of the following 3 examples, set up by department, by type, or by units. In the first example, the binding of documents falls within other departments.

Binding Apportionment (by department)

Humanities	_____
Sciences	_____
Social sciences	_____
Theses and dissertation binding (academic library)	_____
In-house binding supplies and equipment	_____
Total	=======

Documents could also be a separate department and have its own allocation, with the apportionment column subdivided into periodicals and books. The following example is predicated on a first-come, first-served basis and could result in the most efficient unit receiving the bulk of the binding budget.

Binding Apportionment (by type)

Periodicals binding	_____
Book repair and binding	_____
Thesis and dissertation binding (academic library)	_____
Supplies and equipment	_____
Total	=======

Finally, in the third example, the total apportionment has been allocated to each unit (central library or branch libraries). The units can then subdivide the allocations themselves among books, periodicals, and media as best serves their needs. Branch libraries may need relatively small allocations if most of the bound periodical back files are kept in the central library. Also, a library system may elect to divide its periodicals binding budget into current subscription binding and back files binding. Such a division would allow the library to place its binding emphasis where it can best serve the clientele, for example, by stressing the current, heavily used titles, and deemphasizing the least used materials. These previously unbound back files could also be converted to microfilm to save space.

Binding Apportionment (by units)

Central library	_____
Branch library	_____
Supplies and equipment	_____
Total	=======

Periodicals

The periodical portion of the total budget should be allocated among units in as simple a manner as possible.

Because of the sometimes confusing nature of periodical subscriptions, this budget can easily become a headache. Several guidelines, if followed consistently, can eliminate many of the problems. For example, all periodicals should be renewed on the same schedule to eliminate the confusion of variable renewal periods. A calendar-year basis is preferable because it corresponds with most frequently used volume numbering. If this standard renewal period does not correspond to your fiscal year, adjustments will be necessary.

Public libraries, because of the popular nature of their periodicals, may be able to take advantage of the discounts available by placing 2- and 3-year subscriptions. Academic libraries, however, with their preponderance of scholarly titles, usually are not able to take advantage of cheaper multiple-year subscriptions. Keep in mind that multiple-year subscriptions also carry the built in risk that a given title will cease publication midway through the subscription period or that the library may be forced to cancel its subscription before normal expiration. There may then be problems obtaining a refund for the unused portion of the subscription. Having subscriptions placed on a standard renewal cycle allows for easier monitoring and cost projections in a manual system.

With the inflationary characteristics inherent in subscriptions, the less complicated the allocation breakdown, the better for the people administering the funds. Once an allocation system has been devised, whether it be by department, subject, pool fund, or based upon a formula or incremental system, every effort should be made to retain that apportionment scheme. Switching from one scheme to another is not only confusing to everyone involved but also limits management's ability to monitor periodicals accurately over a long period.

One large pool fund is the simplest periodicals budget to administer. Under this arrangement all subscriptions are paid from one fund with no discrimination between subject areas or units for which the subscription is being purchased. One advisable way to modify this pool fund is by setting aside a separate subfund to use for filling in gaps in back files, thus identifying those funds used specifically for maintaining the current collection as distinct from those funds allocated for the development of the existing collection.

There may still be a need for further apportionment of the periodical funds, especially by subject. It is particularly difficult, however, to allocate periodical funds by subject area due to the interdisciplinary nature of so many titles. Some libraries, especially academic libraries, attempt to allocate their periodical budgets by subject area, assigning each periodical title to that subject area or department first requesting the subscription. This is an onerous system to maintain and can often result in attempts by librarians and faculty to cancel periodicals on a whim without regard to the problems such decisions create for other users of that title. Enlist the assistance of your periodical vendor in identifying titles by subject area. Some vendors now have management reports available which group periodical titles by subject area using the Library of Congress classification scheme. Such management reports can be helpful for the library using a manual accounting system and requiring a system of subject allocations.

A more sensible distribution of periodical funds might consist of an arrangement by major subject groupings such as humanities, sciences, and social sciences. These subaccounts reveal some insight into the disbursement of the periodical budget without necessitating the detail required by recording the expenditures of numerous, separate funds. Periodical distribution may also be identified by agency location: central library and branch libraries. Again, the management reports supplied by some periodical vendors can be coded by the library staff itself so that management reports are produced, arranged by major categories, funds, or location. Judicious use of these vendor reports can significantly offset the many disadvantages of a manual accounting system.

In addition to the variety of ways current subscription funds may be allocated, some consideration must be given to establishing new subscriptions. While many libraries have had to cut their allocations for periodical subscriptions or have imposed a freeze on orders for new subscriptions, there are usually ways to establish at least a few new subscriptions. A new subscription fund, albeit small, may still be a factor to take into consideration. However few new subscription orders you may be able to place, keep in mind that these new, ongoing commitments must be built into the existing fund distribution for future budgets.

Individual issues of periodicals have a habit of disappearing while others are mutilated at an alarming rate, so that there is a need to provide a fund for the purchase of these missing issues as soon as possible, before replacement issues are no longer available. Postponement of purchase may result in having to purchase entire volumes rather than single issues or in replacing the missing parts with microform.

The apportionment concepts mentioned thus far may be varied to resemble any one of these 3 patterns, based upon pool fund, category, or location.

Periodical Apportionment (pool fund)

Periodical renewal fund   _____
New subscriptions   _____
Missing issues   _____
Total   _____

or

Periodical Apportionment (by category)

Periodical renewal fund   _____
  Humanities   _____
  Sciences   _____
  Social sciences   _____
New subscriptions   _____
Missing issues   _____
Total   _____

or

Periodical Apportionment (by location)

Periodical renewal fund   _____
  Central library   _____
  Branch A   _____
  Branch B   _____
  Branch C   _____
  Etc.   _____
Missing issues   _____
  Central Library   _____
  Branch A   _____
  Branch B   _____
  Branch C   _____
Total   _____

Although the variations for apportioning funds for periodicals are infinite, the less complicated you keep the allocations, the better for all involved.

When allocating funds for periodicals, you need to be constantly aware of the effect of the inflation rate on periodical prices. Many library periodicals and annuals regularly report the fluctuations in the national inflation rate for periodicals. To find the most current trends you may also want to consult with your major periodical vendors for their latest inflation estimates and forecasts for the coming year. You may also set up your own mechanism for gathering statistics to determine the inflation of past years as it affects your own particular mix of periodical subscriptions. While this does not provide you with an accurate prediction of the rate for the years ahead, it does show you the rates for previous years and provides you with a basis on which to formulate your own estimates.

One simple method for checking your own inflation rate for your library involves making a chart of periodical titles and prices arranged by year (see figure 5).

FIGURE 5. Periodical titles and prices arranged by year.

Title	Price Total 1979/80	First Invoice 1980/81	Price Total 1980/81	% (+ or −)	First Invoice 1981/82	Price Total 1981/82	% (+ or −)	First Invoice 1982/83	Price Total 1982/83	% (+ or −)	% 3 years

In brief, every tenth title is listed, followed by the subscription price for each year of the study. The percent increase is determined in relation to the previous year's costs. However, by having at hand your cost for year one, you can also determine the inflation rate based on the prices of successive years compared to prices listed in that first year of your study. Such a study based on an evaluation of prices for your library's current periodicals will provide invaluable, specific information tied directly to your subscriptions whose collective rate of inflation may be higher or lower than the national averages.

Books

When you are considering book allocations, the number of subaccounts always seems to multiply so quickly that the books portion of the budget has more subaccounts than any other part of the library budget. Purchasing from a single pool fund is possible and often desirable, particularly in smaller libraries. However, most libraries find it necessary to establish at least a few basic subaccounts as a better means of following purchasing patterns as well as aiding in the development of a balanced collection. The subaccounts tend to help enforce purchasing guidelines by providing spending limits in categories which may range from types of book (fiction and nonfiction) to reading levels (adult and juvenile) to location (central library and branches). Firm-order monies may also be allocated by subject areas (English, history, botany, etc.). Within each of

Book Apportionment (by type)	
Fiction	_____
Nonfiction	_____
Biography	_____
Reference	_____
Record collection	_____
Media	_____
Total	========

or

Book Apportionment (by level)	
Adult fiction	_____
Adult nonfiction	_____
Adult biography	_____
Juvenile fiction	_____
Juvenile nonfiction	_____
Juvenile biography	_____
Adult record collection	_____
Juvenile record collection	_____
Juvenile media	_____
Reference	_____
Total	========

or

Book Apportionment (by location)	
Reference total	_____
Central library	_____
Branch A	_____
Branch B	_____
Branch C	_____
Fiction—adult total	_____
Central library	_____
Branch A	_____
Branch B	_____
Branch C	_____
Nonfiction—adult total	_____
Central library	_____
Branch A	_____
Branch B	_____
Branch C	_____
Biography—adult total	_____
Central library	_____
Branch A	_____
Branch B	_____
Branch C	_____
Fiction—juvenile total	_____
Central library	_____
Branch A	_____
Branch B	_____
Branch C	_____
Nonfiction—juvenile total	_____
Central library	_____
Branch A	_____
Branch B	_____
Branch C	_____
Biography—juvenile total	_____
Central library	_____
Branch A	_____
Branch B	_____
Branch C	_____
Records—adult total	_____
Central library	_____
Branch A	_____
Branch B	_____
Branch C	_____
Records—juvenile total	_____
Central library	_____
Branch A	_____
Branch B	_____
Branch C	_____
Media total	_____
Central library	_____
Branch A	_____
Branch B	_____
Branch C	_____
Books and media—grand total	========

these allocation patterns, you may also provide subaccounts for reference and media purchases.

Format of the allocation schedule can vary, but the apportionment pattern you select may resemble one of these divisions, based upon type, level, or location. Note that records and media are included within book allocations in these examples.

Another alternative within the various categories of apportioning is to allocate units rather than dollars. Then the selectors need only keep track of the number rather than dollar value of books they have ordered. A unit allocation system is more likely to be feasible in a public library system than in an academic library, where the cost of scholarly materials, especially in some disciplines, is high.

The subject allocation scheme is the most complex with which to deal. Subjects and consequently accounts are infinite in number. The potential to expand both is limitless. If subject accounts can be tied to academic departments, the account explosion may be lessened somewhat. Allocations for each account may be determined by a formula based upon enrollment, circulation statistics, or other variables. The allocations may also be based upon expenditures in previous years. Whatever subject allocation scheme you elect to use, once it is adopted use it consistently throughout all the allocations. If political pressures lead to changes in some allocations, problems can be anticipated as people from other disciplines learn of the favoritism. Also, once you have devised an apportionment system, you will find it difficult to change the basic method of allocation in future years. An incremental allocation approach is expected; thus, there will be great resistance should you attempt to cut the allocation for a department that has decreasing enrollment.

Book Apportionment (by subject or department)

Botany   _____
Chemistry   _____
English   _____
Geology   _____
Geography   _____
History   _____
Mathematics   _____
Psychology   _____
Sociology   _____
Etc.   _____

_____   _____
_____   _____
_____   _____

Reference   _____
Replacements   _____
Records   _____
Children's literature   _____
Media   _____

When it is possible to increase allocations in a given year, try to tie these increases to average book price increases in subject areas. Annually, reports are published showing the average cost of books in specific subject areas. If your library uses an approval plan, the reports issued by your vendor showing average prices in your selection categories are useful to determine overall cost increases for your library. However, any changes in allocations based on these cost increases should be carefully explained so that favoritism to some subjects is not implied.

Approval Plans, Continuations, and General Guidelines

Approval Plans. Academic libraries and also some public libraries may use approval plans for a portion of their purchasing. Rather than having the books received under such arrangements charged internally to individual subject subaccounts, it is simpler to pay for them out of one pool fund. This avoids having to determine an individual subaccount for each book received. The approval vendor management reports can always supply individual cost figures for each subject category by number of volumes and dollars if this information is needed.

Continuations. Part of the book or periodical funds may be earmarked for continuations or standing orders. As with periodical subscriptions, this continuation fund may be further divided by categories or location or be kept in a single pool fund. An additional subdivision that may be part of the continuation fund may be a portion set aside for continuations that are earmarked for reference books.

The continuation allocation should be designed to accommodate increases in the inflation rate each year. Studies are regularly published in the library literature which indicate national inflation rates for serials. For in-house use, a study similar to the one suggested for periodicals may be useful. One complication which affects determining inflation rates for continuations is that all continuations are not received each year; thus, calculating the proper allocation and estimating the inflation trend accurately can be extremely difficult. The continuation budget may also be subject to periodic cuts or freezes, making regular establishment of new continuations difficult. In some years, it may be possible to budget for new continuations. These are ongoing commitments, however, and must be built into all future allocations along with an appropriate inflation increment.

The continuation fund distribution may resemble the apportionment examples listed for periodicals, with an added category for reference purchases if you need a way to monitor these special purchases. Because of the erratic nature of serial publishing and receipts, it may be desirable to forget the system of subaccounts and use a single pool fund to cover all these purchases.

General Guidelines for Allocations. Most of your bookkeeping activities will revolve around *book* allocations. Once periodical subscriptions are set up, if monitored properly, they continue automatically until cancelled. Each book purchase constitutes a complete transaction with a beginning and an end and includes many possible clerical activities in between. Some of these are related to bookkeeping. With thousands of books being purchased by your library in a given year, these bookkeeping activities can result in numerous time-consuming transactions.

Another area for concern is equipment since large sums of money may be spent for individual items: accounting machines, electronic typewriters, postage machines, and cash registers. Whether or not there is an allocation system for equipment, someone within the organization should review equipment requests so that typewriter replacements are rotated, major purchases are not inadvertently duplicated, and only needed equipment is purchased.

Your fund allocations should be available as early as possible in the fiscal year. Selectors will want to start purchasing books as soon as money is available. Deadlines for ordering should also be announced early in the year to enable selectors to plan their purchasing throughout the year. Purchasing should also be planned so that allocations can be expended within the fiscal year for which monies were allocated, even if the carryover of funds from one fiscal year to the next is permitted. Carrying large balances of unexpended funds can often be interpreted as a signal that too much money is being appropriated.

Allocation reports should be issued on a regular basis. If selectors know the report schedule, they can avoid making frequent requests for the fund balances.

ENCUMBERING

An encumbrance is "an anticipated expenditure, evidenced by a contract or purchase order."[1]

Why bother to encumber? Why not simply send out the orders, whether for a supply item or a book purchase? Why keep any records at all before you actually expend funds? In some library systems, encumbering is a legal requirement and a signature may even be required on the purchase order guaranteeing

that funds are indeed available for the purchase of the goods. Committing funds for the acquisitions of goods in advance of the actual purchase means it is unnecessary to worry about cancelling orders due to the lack of funds or juggling funds at the last minute in order to avoid an overdraft.

The Format

Encumbrance documents for goods and services for the operation of the library may take the form of quotations, encumbering requisitions, official purchase orders, work orders, or even estimated figures based on past experience. Encumbrance documents for books and periodicals may be purchase orders issued to one vendor for several titles or may be individual purchase orders for each item ordered. Single purchase orders for many items from the same vendor often work well for supply or equipment items. With books and periodicals, however, an individual purchase order for each title is more appropriate. Although several titles can be ordered on one purchase order, that purchase order must then be kept open until all titles are received.

Figures 6 and 7 present examples of a purchase order for multiple items and of a purchase order for a single item, specifically for an individual book.

If the 3" × 5" "multiples" commonly used for ordering materials are treated as the official library purchase order, each with a unique control number, then each purchase order can be cleared upon receipt of the book or media. The use of these multiple-part forms, which results in a single purchase order for each title, means more encumbering activity, but also allows unused funds to be released quickly for other encumbrances and expenditures.

The method of encumbering depends upon the system used internally. The actual encumbering document selected should be dated and include a vendor name, a control number, and the list price. Encumbering the list price provides a margin for any additional future charges such as postage or handling. In addition, encumbering for full list price eliminates the need to estimate in advance anticipated discounts, while at the same time allowing some additional funds to be held in reserve for those items purchased for net or for increased charges. If you prefer to encumber a discounted price, try to use a standard average discounted price so time is not wasted figuring individual prices for each purchase.

In a manual system, the encumbrance document must arrive at the desk of the account clerk or other person charged with the encumbering function as soon after preparation of the order as possible. The encum-

[1]Eric L. Kohler. *A Dictionary for Accountants*, 5th ed. (Englewood Cliffs, NJ: Prentice Hall, 1975), p. 192.

FIGURE 6. A multiple-item purchase order.

Purchase Order

Name, Address and
Telephone Number

Purchase Order No.
(Control Numer)

TO:

(vendor name and address)

Date _____

Item	Description	Quantity	Unit Price	Total

State any special terms and conditions
of purchase for individual institution

By _____

Title _____

FIGURE 7. Two types of multiple-part purchase orders used for single-item orders such as a book or periodical subscription.

PURCHASE ORDER NUMBER	ORDER DATE	FUND NUMBER	LIB./AGY./LEV.
CLASS NUMBER		L.C.C.N.	REPORT LINE ITEM NO

QTY.	
COST	
DATE RECD.	ORDER QUANTITY BY AGENCY AND LEVEL

ACCT. NO:

ISBN:

LIST PRICE:

VENDOR:

Commercial form used by Baker & Taylor LIBRIS (automated acquisitions) customers.[*]

FUND	ISN	ORDER DATE	VENDOR	LIBRARY ORDER NO.
				L 53066

TITLE - AUTHOR - EDITION - PUBLISHER - DATE

PRICE   NO. COPIES

DATE RECEIVED

COST

INVOICE NO. & DATE

LIBRARY
PURCHASE ORDER

ORDER NUMBER MUST APPEAR ON ALL SHIPMENTS AND INVOICES.

INVOICE IN TRIPLICATE. REPORT IN 120 DAYS OR CONSIDER CANCELLED.

PLEASE RETURN PINK COPY WITH BOOK.

ACQUISITION DEPT.-MIAMI UN. LIBRARY, OXFORD, OHIO 45056

Form developed for use in manual acquisitions system.

---

[*]Used by permission of Baker & Taylor.

brance document should be processed expeditiously by the clerk, so that the order can be mailed and the copies filed.

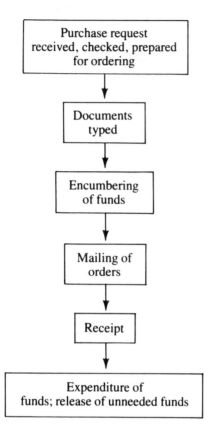

Blanket Encumbering

Blanket encumbering can also be used as a means of holding funds until you are ready to expend. A blanket encumbrance prepared at the beginning of the year would be issued to "various vendors" and would be made out for the full amount of the allocation (see figure 8). Use of a blanket encumbrance may enable you to issue purchase orders against this blanket encumbrance throughout the fiscal year. As goods are received, they are then charged against this blanket encumbrance until the full value of the encumbrance has been dispensed.

Setting Up an Encumbering System

Most of the encumbering in a manual system is for materials to be purchased such as books, periodicals, and media. Any system for encumbering should be straightforward and easily maintained. It should provide audit trails that can be followed from encumbering the initial order through to the corresponding expendi-

ture. Checks for accuracy should be easy to make and consistency in procedures should be a basic goal. The set of books you maintain for a library's manual accounting system may not resemble those which you might set up for a formal bookkeeping course. Instead, the records should be designed to serve your needs.

If you are establishing a manual bookkeeping system and need to set up an encumbering procedure, the system described in the next few pages could serve your purposes. The procedure is described in terms of book orders with individual purchase order numbers for each book. However, the steps could be modified to fit different materials and purchase orders that are designed for multiple items.

In the sample system described, the order multiples are prepared and separated with the copy to be used for encumbering and later for paying going to the account clerk. While encumbering is taking place, the copies to be mailed can be placed in envelopes and remaining copies filed. Then as soon as encumbering is completed (confirming that sufficient funds are available to support the purchase) vendor copies can be mailed.

Encumbering: A Sample Procedure

Before beginning the process of encumbering, first complete these preliminary steps:

1. Group the forms by fund number.
2. Within each fund, put the forms in order by date, last date at the back.
3. Be sure that the control or purchase order numbers within each fund are in order.

When preparing the orders using individual purchase orders, group those going to the same vendor together so that purchase order numbers will be consecutive (see figure 9).

Once the documents are arranged, locate the fund pages and prepare to post the orders (see figure 10).

1. Post order date from multiple to date column on ledger sheet.
2. Post vendor name from multiple to vendor column on ledger sheet.
3. Post the order control number from the multiple to the ledger sheet column marked "order number."
4. Post the price listed on the multiple to the ledger sheet column marked "encumbered."
5. After completing step 4, go back and place a check mark (✓) before the price on the multiple.

FIGURE 8. Example of a requisition for a blanket encumbrance.

THIS SECTION FOR BUSINESS OFFICE USE															
2	3	4	5 - 7	8 - 9	10 - 11	12 - 14	15	33 - 39	40 - 44	52 - 57	58 - 61				A M O U N T
FD GRP	ACCT TYPE	MAJ FUNC	LOC. S. FUNC. FUND NO.	MAJ ACT	MIN ACT	STAND OBJECT	Y R	INVOICE NO.	VENDOR NO.	P.O. NO.	DATE MO. DAY YR.				

REQUISITION

MIAMI UNIVERSITY
OXFORD, OHIO

REQUISITION DATE
October 10, 1980

DEPARTMENT
Library

DEPT. REQ. NO.
L-1489

DATE WANTED

ACCOUNT TO BE CHARGED
Library B & P Books – Standing Orders

NAME OF PREFERRED VENDOR (IF ANY) (16-32)
▶**Various Vendors**

ADDRESS
▶

▶

QUANTITY	UNIT	ITEM (GIVE COMPLETE SPECIFICATIONS)	UNIT PRICE	AMOUNT
		Blanket encumbrance for the purchase of books. 1980-81		114,000.00
		DO NOT MAIL VENDOR COPY.		

RECEIVED

DELIVER TO _____ ROOM NO. _____ BLDG. _____

DEAN OR ADM. OFFICER

REQUESTED BY **Jennifer Cargill**

DIRECTOR OF PURCHASES

APPROVED **Brian Alley**

HEAD OF DEPT.

COMPTROLLER

MU NO. 6051

ACCOUNTING COPY

FIGURE 9. Individual purchase orders to be grouped by fund type, number, and in numerical sequence.

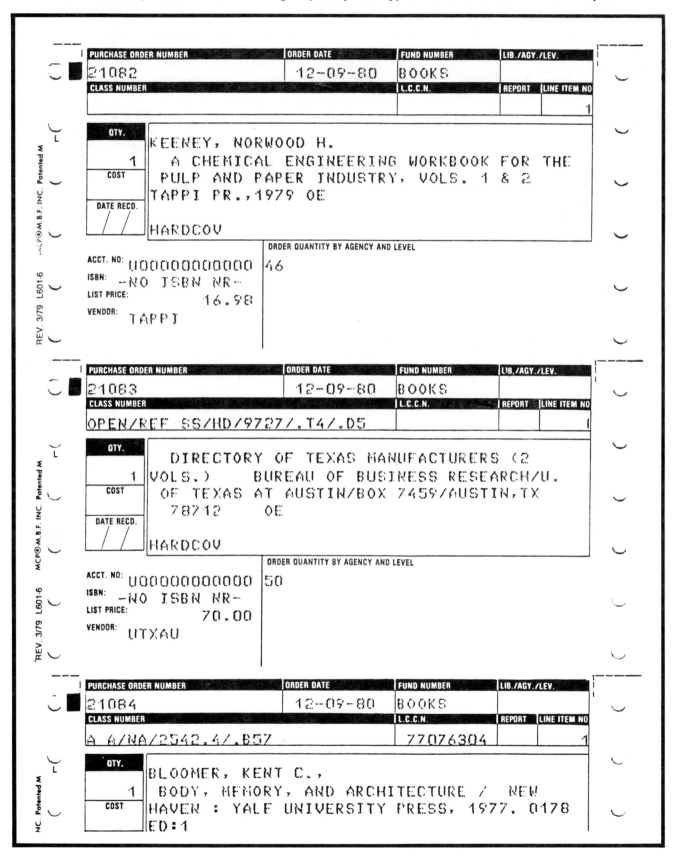

FIGURE 10. Posted entries in an example of encumbering procedure.

BOOKS

Page _____ 1 _____

Year _____ 1980 -81 _____

Allocation $200.00   Fund LITERATURE   # _____ 07 _____

	Date	Vendor	1 Order #	2 Encum.	3 Expend.	4 Total Encum.	5 Total Expend.	6 Unencum. Balance	
		Totals from previous page						200 -	
1	7/1	PEN.CO.	43716	10 -		10 -		190 -	1
2	7/2	SOCKENZE	43740	750		1750		18250	2
3	7/3	BLACKSTONE	43792	1195					3
4	"	"	43794	2869		5814		14186	4
5	7/5	BARTON	43795	6 -					5
6	"	"	43796	2 -					6
7	"	"	43797	2 -					7
8	"	"	43798	2 -					8
9	"	"	43799	2 -					9
10	"	"	43800	2 -		7414		12586	10
11	7/7	U. OF QUEENSLAND	43808	1290		8704		11296	11
12	"	BOYORS	43809	15 -		10204		9796	12
13	7/8	NORTH	43811	10 -		11204		8796	13
14	7/13	AMS	43820	55 -		16704		3296	14
15									15
16									16
17									17
18									18
19									19
20									20
21									21
22									22
23									23
24									24
25									25
26									26
27									27
28									28
29									29
30									30
31									31
32									32
33									33
34									34
35									35
36									36
37									37
38									38
	PAGE TOTAL								

Post all orders in each fund group before you go on to the next fund. When you complete posting for a given fund group, add all individual prices you have just posted in the encumbered column. This total is added to the running total in the "total encumbered" column. Be sure that the new running total is posted in the total encumbered column on the same line (level with and opposite) as the last encumbrance you posted.

Subtract the total encumbered column from the original allocation. The result is your free balance. Enter this new free balance in the unencumbered balance column on the same line as the last entry.

When you have posted all encumbrances on a given fund and have calculated the new free balance, check your ledger for accuracy as follows:

1. Add up the individual prices on the multiples you have just posted and add the resulting sum to the free balance. The result should equal the *previous* free balance.
2. To check someone else who has made entries, or yourself, subtract the encumbered amounts on each individual slip. The result should equal the previous encumbered figure. Enter the new free balance and add up the amounts on the encumbered slips. This figure should equal the previous free balance.

If all is accurate, place a check mark by each figure to indicate you have double-checked the arithmetic.

Once encumbering has been completed and double-checked, the account clerk should alert the ordering unit that the orders may be released. The person responsible for the funds, whether they are supply, equipment, or materials, will know at any given time exactly how much uncommitted money is available.

Keep in mind that at this stage we are discussing a *sample encumbering procedure.* You may adapt these procedures for your own manual bookkeeping system.

EXPENDING

Thus far we have concentrated on encumbering funds prior to placing orders, ensuring that those funds will be available when goods are received. Now we consider the expending process. Expending involves the actual disbursement of funds for materials received. Why bother to record these internally if another office within the parent organization is actually issuing the checks? Why not simply rely on their reports?

If another office is actually expending the funds, the interval between the reports it issues may be so long as to negate the value of those reports by the time you receive them. By relying upon those reports to keep up-to-date, you could commit funds that the reports showed as free balances but which in reality had already been expended. The only way to have an accurate reading of account status in situations such as this is to keep your own expenditure records. In this way you will know at all times exactly which funds are actually uncommitted.

Establishing Expenditure Records

Assuming you have been keeping internal records as you encumber funds and mail orders, it is a simple process to build upon your bookkeeping system by establishing a set of expenditure records. For each recorded encumbrance, there should be a corresponding expenditure unless an encumbered item is cancelled. Actual expenditures should be recorded only after the material is received and the true cost is known. The actual cost of the received item should include any discounts or additional charges. Expenditures should be posted to the same fund in which the monies were originally encumbered, thus giving that fund the benefit of any discounts as well as ensuring that it will absorb additional charges.

The same documents used for encumbering may also be used for expending. The price is recorded on the document along with the date received. Actual bookkeeping routines for expending depend upon the internal system used, but expenditures should not be recorded until after the goods have been received and checked in order to be sure that what is received matches the purchase order and the invoice.

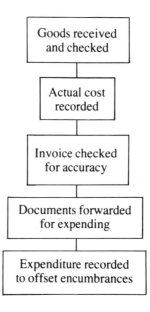

For any goods received, the cost should be posted in the account books. For those items ordered on individual multiples (which may be considered de facto purchase orders), the actual cost can be recorded directly on the part of the multiple which you used originally as the encumbrance document. This posting routine is especially applicable to book multiples. When you post costs, don't forget to record the date of receipt and the invoice number. This process provides a clear audit trail and simplifies follow-up should it become necessary.

Most of the library expending transactions involve books. The procedure described in the next few pages completes the encumbering procedure already described. This simple, straightforward method allows both discounts and additional charges to be tied directly to the appropriate funds.

Once the books have been received and the cost, date of receipt, and invoice number have been recorded, the expenditure slips (formerly the encumbrance slips) are delivered to the account clerk or the person responsible for the posting.

Expending: A Sample Procedure

Before any expending takes place, you must complete some preliminary steps:

1. Group expenditure slips by fund number.
2. Put the slips in order by date within each fund.
3. Be sure the control or purchase order numbers within each fund are in order.

Once you have arranged the documents in order, you can begin expending. Follow the same basic format used for encumbering (see figure 11).

1. For each slip, locate the original encumbrance posting using the purchase order or control number.
2. Enter the cost from the multiple in the expended column opposite the amount already encumbered for that item. Process all multiples in that fund in the same way.
3. After posting all cost figures in a single fund group, turn to the last entry for the fund. On the next line, in the date column, record the received date.
4. On the same line, in the vendor column, write "pd." along with the purchase order or control numbers for those slips you are expending.
5. Total the original encumbered figures (available on these slips) and record this total in the encumbered column in parentheses and precede it with a minus sign: (-115.00).

6. Subtract this amount from the total encumbered column so that you now have a new total encumbered figure.
7. Total the actual costs from your slips to get the amount you want to expend and post the resulting figure in the total expended column.
8. By subtracting the new total encumbered and total expended figures, you will now have a free balance to enter in the unencumbered balance column.

Place check marks by the expended amounts on each slip as a reminder that you have processed each slip. Similarly, as you recheck each fund balance for accuracy, check marks by each total figure in your account ledger will indicate that each total has been verified.

To make a quick check of your or someone else's postings:

1. Add the encumbrances on the slips to the new total encumbered figure. The results should give you the previous total encumbered figure.
2. Subtract the paid amounts from the new total expended figure. The result should provide you with the previous total expended figure.
3. Take the present unencumbered balance, subtract all the encumbrances and then add the expenditures to get the previous unencumbered balance.

By placing check marks by each column as you go, you'll know which figures you have verified for accuracy.

Your simple manual system for internal recordkeeping has now provided you with a method of offsetting your encumbrances by posting expenditures.

Cancellations

Occasionally, you may find it necessary to cancel an encumbrance. If you are using the recordkeeping procedure previously described, your cancelling should be done like this:

1. Arrange the slips to be cancelled in order by fund number.
2. Place the multiples in order (within each fund) according to order control number, with the lowest number on top.
3. Take the first multiple and match it to the corresponding entry in the encumbered column. Use the multiple order number and date to help you match the records.
4. Write the word "Cancelled" in the expended column. Place a check mark on the multiple you have

FIGURE 11. Posted entries in an example of expending funds.

BOOKS

Page 1

Year 1980-81

Allocation $200.00   Fund LITERATURE   # 07

	Date	Vendor	1 Order #	2 Encum.	3 Expend.	4 Total Encum.	5 Total Expend.	6 Unencum. Balance	
		Totals from previous page							
1	7/1	REN CO.	43716	10-	950	10-		190-	1
2	7/2	SOCKENZE	43740	750	750	1750		18250	2
3	7/3	BLACKSTONE	43792	1195	1015				3
4	"	"	43794	2869	30-	5814		14186	4
5	7/6	BARTON	43795	6-	6-				5
6	"	"	43796	2-	2-				6
7	"	"	43797	2-	2-				7
8	"	"	43798	2-	2-				8
9	"	"	43799	2-	2-				9
10	"	"	43800	2-	2-	7414		12586	10
11	7/7	U. OF QUEENSLAND	43808	1290	10-	8704		11296	11
12	7/7	BOYARS	43809	15-	10-	10204		9796	12
13	7/8	NORTH	43811	10-	750	11204		8796	13
14	7/13	AMS	43820	55-		16704		3296	14
15	8/1	Pd.43716, 43740,							15
16		43792, 43794,							16
17		43795-43800,							17
18		43808, 43809,							18
19		43811		(11204)		5500	10065	4435	19

PAGE TOTAL

FIGURE 12. Full month's fiscal activity.

BOOKS

Page _____ 1 _____

Year __ 1980 - 81 __

Allocation __ $7500.00 __   Fund __ BOOKS __   # _____ 12 _____

	Date	Vendor	1 Order #	2 Encum.	3 Expend.	4 Total Encum.	5 Total Expend.	6 Unencum. Balance	
	Totals from previous page								
1	7/1	B&T	43788	20 -	CANCELLED				1
2	7/1	BELOX	43789	8270	11025				2
3	7/1	"	43790	775	1230				3
4	7/1	"	43791	1447	1575	12492			4
5	7/2	B&T	43891	75 -	CANCELLED				5
6	7/2	"	43892	1225	CANCELLED	21217			6
7	7/2	ROUTLEDGE	44004	35 -	3173				7
8	7/2	ST. MARTINS	44005	1695	623	26412			8
9	7/11	B&T	44050	995	846	27407			9
10	7/12	"	44051	1495	919				10
11	7/12	"	44052	3000	1845	31902			11
12	7/13	CANC. 43788		(20 -)		29902			12
13	7/16	CARRIER PIGEON	44335	1132	CANCELLED	31034			13
14	7/18	XEROX	44413	950	18 -				14
15	7/18	KAMKIN	44420	2 -	2 -				15
16	7/28	GEOLIUS	44435	16 -	18 -				16
17	7/18	"	44436	20 -	20 -	35784			17
18	7/20	KAMKIN	44495	790	790				18
19	7/20	"	44497	290	290				19
20	7/20	"	44500	350	350				20
21	7/20	"	44501	1295	325				21
22	7/20	"	44502	370	375				22
23	7/20	"	44503	250	250				23
24	7/20	"	44504	550	550				24
25	7/20	"	44505	350	350				25
26	7/20	"	44520	6 -	6 -	40629		709371	26
27	8/3	CANC. 44335		(1132)		39497		710503	27
28	8/3	BELOX	44829	1144	570	40641		709359	28
29	8/6	B&T	44861	38 -	38 -				29
30			44862	1095	673				30
31			44863	445	243				31
32			44865	1250	1081				32
33			44866	650	CANCELLED	47881		702119	33
34	8/7	RJ. 44004		(35 -)		44381	3173	702446	34
35									35
36									36
37									37
38									38
	PAGE TOTAL								

just posted by the word "Cancelled" so you'll know you have made a cancellation.

5. Check to make sure that the price on the multiple is the same as the figure in the encumbered column.
6. Write the cancellation date on the next line after the last entry for the fund.
7. Note "Canc." and the order number(s) in the vendor column.
8. Record in parentheses the total amount being cancelled (-115.00) in the encumbered column.
9. Subtract this amount from the total encumbered column, recording a new total encumbered figure.
10. Subtract the total encumbered and the total expended figures from the original allocation to obtain a new, unencumbered balance. Then enter that balance in that column.

Figure 12 reflects a full month's activity on one sub-account, showing cancellations, encumbrances, and expenditures. Activity on subsequent pages led to some postings in Figure 12.

PURCHASING ALTERNATIVES

Often it is impossible to take the time to initiate a formal requisition or purchase order for goods or services. This may occur when equipment repair is needed, goods are available locally and are needed quickly, or goods have been acquired already and only payment is necessary. In such instances the formal requisition or voucher serves as a request for payment or a confirmation of receipt so payment may be initiated. In instances where all of your encumbering is done internally without the benefit of official encumbering, the initiation of payment will be the only time the parent organization becomes aware of the financial transaction.

Using Temporary Purchase Orders

Many institutions use temporary purchase orders to facilitate local or emergency purchases. The local vendor may receive the temporary purchase order number by phone and then cite it on all invoices or other fiscal documents. Whenever using a temporary purchase order number, you should keep a log of the numbers, including the vendors used, the materials purchased, and the total cost. Amounts should be encumbered against the fund involved, so that when it is time to expend monies an audit trail is obvious.

Using Central Purchasing

Requisitions may be submitted to another office within the organization for the purchase of equipment or large items for which the library lacks the authority to purchase directly. These requisitions include the specifications for the product or services, the approximate cost, a possible vendor, and the directions for delivery. The central purchasing office then proceeds with its normal purchase routine, perhaps obtaining quotes from several vendors or investigating the purchasing alternatives if a better product or price is anticipated.

In instances where prepayment for goods or services is required, purchasing requisitions designed for prepayment may be used. A word of caution: This is an area in which some unscrupulous vendors take advantage of a library's willingness to comply with a request for advance payment. If you are not sure of your vendor, ask for references or solicit assistance from your purchasing agent. Figure 13 is a sample prepayment form. In many cases, of course, the standard requisition can be modified for use as a prepayment form by typing in the word "prepayment" and attaching any documen-

FIGURE 13. Internal form used as request for prepayment.

Request for Prepayment

Library Department _____

Library Name _____

Date _____

Documentation of reason for prepayment is attached.

Amount _____

Account to charge _____

Make check payable to: _____

_____

_____

Send to: ☐ Library department
☐ Vendor with order form attached
☐ See special instruction below

Approved _____

tation or special instructions. The type of form used depends upon the degree of formality required by the parent organization.

Figures 14 and 15 are examples of requisition forms used that can be used to requisition different goods and services.

FIGURE 14. Example of requisition submitted to another office within the organization.

Requisition				
Library Name				
Address				
Phone Number				

Date _____

Requisition Number _____

To:

Account Charged

Ship to: ☐ Central Receiving
☐ Library

Quantity	Item(s) Ordered Description	Unit Price	Total Price

Approved by _____

FIGURE 15. Example of supplies/services requisition.

Requisition for Supplies or Services

Department requisition number _____   Date _____

Please furnish the items listed below to the following library department: _____
_____

Charge to: _____   Delivery address: _____

When needed: _____   _____
_____

Quantity Requested	Unit	Description of Articles or Services	Unit Price	Amount

Instructions

1. Number requisitions consecutively.
2. Retain copy for department files.

Signature _____

Approved by _____
(Department head or authorized agent)

Petty Cash Records

Finally, if petty cash is used within the organization, to purchase small items or materials available locally, recordkeeping is always necessary to monitor it. Such expenditures may be monitored through the use of a log (figure 16) or by the collection receipts. Anyone using petty cash must obtain receipts for every purchase made.

Petty cash vouchers may be used to support cash payments to an individual. The recipient should always acknowledge receipt of the cash by signing the voucher. A copy goes to the individual receiving the money and a copy is kept by the library. When the petty cash fund is low, gathering the library copies of the vouchers and totaling them will provide documentation for the request to replenish the fund.

PAYMENTS AND PAYMENT RECORDS

When documents are issued to initiate payment or to support the issuance of a check, a record of the transaction should be kept. These payment records must correspond to the amount of monies paid out of the library accounts. Why bother with keeping internal records? Why not rely upon the report issued by the financial office or the bank statement received each month? Just as you would have no idea of the status of your own personal checking account balance unless you recorded the checks as they were issued, you will have no accurate estimate of the library account balance if regular payment records are not kept. The report from a central office or library bank account statement, in addition to covering several days or weeks, reflects only those transactions which have actually passed through the office or bank. In the meantime, the library could have intitiated large numbers of additional payments, payments not recorded on the official central accounting reports or statements.

Requests for Payment

The institution or organization of which the library is a part may deal with payment initiation in any number of ways.

1. The invoices may be approved after receipt of the goods and then sent to the business office for payment.

2. The invoices may be sent to the business office by the vendor and the library is then required to notify the business office that payment may be made. Problems often arise at this step, especially if payments should be automatic without the use of some fail-safe mechanism by which the library informs the business office that goods were indeed received.

Petty Cash Voucher

Library Name

Number _____   Date _____

Paid to _____

For _____

_____

_____

Amount _____

Received _____   Approved _____

FIGURE 16. A petty cash log.

		Petty Cash Log Library Name Instructions: Record all deposits into the petty cash fund and withdrawals from the fund in sequence.		
Date	Paid to	Description	Amount	Authorized by

3. A requisition or voucher requesting payment may then be prepared by the library, with approved invoices attached. All these documents are sent to the business office for payment. Approval of the invoices is indicated by a stamp on the invoice.

Library Name

Goods or services were received in good condition except as noted on invoice.

P.O. _____

Signature _____

Date _____

Approved for payment _____

---

4. Many libraries prepare and mail their own checks after approving the invoice for payment internally.

Maintaining Audit Trails

Whatever form the request for payment phase takes, certain records must be maintained both to satisfy auditing requirements and as a mechanism for providing internal checks and balances. If invoices are simply approved and then forwarded to another office for actual payment, a log should be kept showing that invoices have been sent. Copies of these invoices must be retained by the library. The invoice journal or log can consist of nothing more than a listing arranged by invoice in order of release for payment, or by vendor, by fund, or a variation of these. If the invoices are mailed directly to the business office by the vendor and you are required to alert that office when invoices may be paid, the log you keep will serve as a checklist showing which invoices were approved for payment and when.

Invoice Journal
(arranged by date released for payment)

Date of Release	Vendor	Invoice Number	Invoice Date	Amount	Fund/Account
7-26	Bow	T47864	7-15	17.68	Supplies
7-27	Presto	5758	7-20	50.29	Equipment
7-27	Blackstone	148765810	7-3	117.20	Books

Invoice Journal
(arranged by vendor)
Bow Co.

Date of Release	Invoice Number	Invoice Date	Amount	Fund
7-8	T34826	7-1	10.20	Supplies
7-15	T39052	7-3	29.10	Supplies
7-26	T47864	7-15	17.68	Supplies

Invoice Journal (arranged by fund) Books				
Date of Release	Vendor	Invoice Number	Invoice Date	Amount
7-15	Plain	148	7-1	52.10
7-18	Kerr	58274	6-20	102.50
7-27	Blackstone	148765810	7-3	117.20

Invoice Journal (arranged by fund catagories)						
Date	Vendor	Invoice	Books	Periodicals	Supplies	Equipment
7-8	Bow	T34826			10.20	
7-15	Bow	T39052			29.10	
7-15	Plain	148	52.10			
7-18	Kerr	58274	102.50			
7-26	Bow	T47864			17.68	
7-27	Presto	5758				50.29

Preparation of Payment Requisitions and Vouchers

When a library prepares its own payment requisitions or vouchers, those documents must be prepared carefully with full account information noted. They may then be recorded in the log or account journal. Several steps are important to keep in mind:

1. The documents should be consecutively numbered. This provides you with a control number which may be used to locate missing documents or to identify a paticular transaction. A simple, automatic hand-numbering machine is sufficient to generate the control numbers, or you may type them in, making sure to keep the numbers in sequence.

2. The official account from which monies should be deducted must be indicated. Always follow the correct format for the account name, including any distinctive account numbering or coding.

3. The vendor should be correctly listed, using the address where payments are to be directed if that address is different from the order fulfillment office.

4. Provide the invoice number, date, and the exact amount to be paid in dollars and cents. If conversion from a foreign currency is necessary, always use the same conversion source, and indicate the conversion date on the invoice or payment requisition.

5. The authorizing signature(s) should be clearly displayed. These signature(s) authorize payment to be made on the basis of an approved invoice. Any variations on the use of authorizing signatures resulting from staff changes, vacation, or prolonged absences should be brought to the attention of the business office before they receive the payment documents.

FIGURE 17. A requisition form.

2	3	4	5 - 7	8 - 9	10 - 11	12 - 14	15	33 - 39	40 - 44	52 - 57	58 - 61			AMOUNT
											MO.	DAY	YR	
FD GRP	ACCT TYPE	MAJ FUNC	LOC. S. FUNC. FUND NO.	MAJ ACT	MIN ACT	STAND OBJECT	Y R	INVOICE NO.	VENDOR NO.	P.O. NO.	DATE			

THIS SECTION FOR BUSINESS OFFICE USE

REQUISITION

MIAMI UNIVERSITY
OXFORD, OHIO

REQUISITION DATE

DEPARTMENT   DEPT. REQ. NO.   DATE WANTED

ACCOUNT TO BE CHARGED

NAME OF PREFERRED VENDOR (IF ANY) (16-32)
▶

ADDRESS
▶

▶

QUANTITY	UNIT	ITEM (GIVE COMPLETE SPECIFICATIONS)	UNIT PRICE	AMOUNT

RECEIVED

DELIVER TO _____
            ROOM NO.   BLDG.   DEAN OR ADM. OFFICER

REQUESTED BY _____   DIRECTOR OF PURCHASES

APPROVED _____
            HEAD OF DEPT.   COMPTROLLER

MU. NO. 6051

ACCOUNTING COPY

Once the requisition or payment voucher (see figures 17 and 18) has been prepared, the account clerk must double-check all these steps before actually forwarding the document for payment. Sometimes a check must be issued to accompany a particular document, such as payment of an honorarium, payment for other services rendered, or payment of registration fees. In such instances, when payment is due immediately, a request for a check form (figure 19) accompanies the documentation.

FIGURE 18. A payment voucher.

<table>
<tr><td colspan="6" align="center">Invoice-Voucher
Library Name
Address</td></tr>
<tr>
<td>Seller's Certification

I hereby certify that the goods, merchandise, wares, or services listed below have met all the required standards set forth in the purchasing contract and are proper charges and that payment has not been received.</td>
<td colspan="2">Vendor Number

Vendor/Payee and Address</td>
<td colspan="3">Voucher Number _____
Voucher Date _____
Account Code Number _____
Invoice Number _____
Invoice Date _____</td>
</tr>
<tr>
<td align="center">Description of Articles or Services</td>
<td align="center">Quantity</td>
<td align="center">Units</td>
<td colspan="2" align="center">Unit Price</td>
<td align="center">Amount</td>
</tr>
<tr><td></td><td></td><td></td><td colspan="2"></td><td></td></tr>
<tr>
<td rowspan="3">For Library Use Only</td>
<td colspan="3" align="right">Subtotal</td>
<td></td>
</tr>
<tr><td colspan="3" align="right">Discounts</td><td></td></tr>
<tr><td colspan="3" align="right">Total Amount</td><td></td></tr>
<tr>
<td colspan="2">The merchandise or service billed above has been received and complies with our specification or request.</td>
<td colspan="4">Certification of Receiving Agency
It is hereby certified that the services or material represented in this voucher were received or authorized, that the amount is correct and hereby approved for payment.</td>
</tr>
<tr>
<td colspan="2">Received by _____

Date _____</td>
<td colspan="4">Approved _____

Date _____</td>
</tr>
<tr><td colspan="6" align="center">Copy 1</td></tr>
</table>

FIGURE 19. A request for a check form.

Request for Check
(complete in full)

Library Name
Address

Date _____

Department _____   Code _____

Make check payable to _____   Amount of check $ _____

_____

Details of transaction _____

_____

_____

Attach any available documentation pertaining to this transaction

Signature—Original Requisitioner   Send Check to: _____

_____   _____

Approval Signature

_____   _____

Payment Records

If payment requisitions or vouchers are prepared by the library and sent to the business office, a log or journal should be maintained along with a file containing copies of all requisitions sent (see following chart). The requisitions will have been numbered sequentially and these numbers are the ones to list in your journal rather than the invoice numbers. Such a requisition ledger might use the following format.

Figures 20 and 21 are examples of a payment requisition ledger showing initiation of payments over a period of time. Such records are needed only if the library prepares its own requisitions or vouchers.

Date	Vendor	Requisition Number	Books	Standing Orders	Periodicals	Total Books	Total Standing Orders	Total Periodicals
7-1	Taylor	1001			1407.90			
7-1	Blackstone	1002			602.06			2009.96
7-1	Taylor	1003	25.00			25.00		2009.96
7-3	ALA	1004		4.50		25.00	4.50	2009.96

FIGURE 20. Example of payment record for books.

Library Books & Periodicals
BOOK Requisitions

Page _____
Year _____

	Date	Vendor	Req. #	1 Books	2 Non Gather. Black-well	3 Non Gather. B&T	4 Standing Order	5 Gather.	6	7 Total Expend. Books	8 Total Expend. Non BHB	9 Total Expend. Non B&T	10 Total Expend. STO	11 Total Expend. Gather.
		Totals from previous page												
1	10/16	UNIV. SERIAS & OK. EXCHANGE	6156	10626										
2	"	HEW & CO.	6157	4130										
3	"	F.W. FANON	6159	846-	See below									
4	"	TECHNICAL SUCS. NEWSLETTER	6162	5-										
5	"	ASSOC. SCIENTIAC PUB.	6164				14666			49856	Ø	Ø	14666	Ø
6	10/17	GISTON-HOMAN, INC.	6191	970										
7	"	AMERICAN PUBL. INC.	6192	370-										
8	"	G.H. BLACKWELL	6193	504										
9	"	GARRY MANN	6194	4-										
10	"	MARCEL GRANCHETAU	6195	6054										
11	"	PAUL H. BROOKS	6196	1776										
12	"	CTR. FOR HUMANITIES	6197	8996										
13	"	COLLEGE BD. PUBL. ORDERS	6198	1544										
14	"	COLLEGE PUBL.	6199	24182										
15	"	COMPOSERS RECORDINGS	1500	928										
16	"	CONGRESSIONAL QUARTERLY	1501	845										
17	"	EDISON RECORD CLEARANCE	1502	11867										
18	"	EDUCATIONAL IMAGES	1503	12908										
19	"	EDUCATIONAL SOLUTIONS	1504	1215										
20	"	ENCYCLOPEDIA BRIT. EDUC.	1505	391-										
21	"	EVERGATE MEDIA INC.	1506	6103										
22	"	FERALS MODERN GUIDES	1507	59										
23	"	THEODORE FRONT	1508	31701										
24	"	GALE RESEARCH CO.	1509	6275										
25	"	GOODYEAR PUBL. CO.	1510	1976										
26	"	G.K. HALL	1511	18786										
27	"	HARPER & ROW	1512	6857										
28	"	HASTINGS HOUSE PUBL.	1513	1359						324480	Ø	Ø	14666	Ø

Different requisition numbers (6000s) represent a group of periodical orders charged against book funds.

FIGURE 21. Example of payment record for other library purchases.

Page _____

Year _____

Library Other Expense Requisitions

Date	Vendor	Req. # (1)	Contract (2)	Postage (3)	Miscellaneous (4)	Supply (5)	Thesis Binding (6)	Total Expend. Contract (7)	Total Expend. Postage (8)	Total Expend. Misc. (9)	Total Expend. Supply (10)	Total Expend. Thesis Bind. (11)
	Totals from previous page											
6/9	STANDARD REGISTER	001										
7/1	EL-BEE	002				9.84 8/5						
7/1	ACCTS. FOR MICROFILM	003				(660)		ø	ø ø	ø	(660)	ø
	SEE	005										
	"	004										
	"	005										
	"	006										
	"	007										
	"	008										
	"	009										
	"	010										
		011										
7/1	PITNEY BOWES	012	45-									
	GUS	013										
	"	014										
7/1	XEROX CORP.	015	113.14									
"	OXFORD HDWR. CORP.	016			6.9							
"	A.B. DICK CORP.	017	858-									
"	SCOT BUS. MACHINES	018	104-									
"	PITNEY BOWES	019		134-								
"	SCOT BUS. MACHINES	020			38-							
"	A.B. DICK CORP.	021	94.54									
"	XEROX CORP.	022	119.24									
"	OCLC	023										
"	FLOSS OFF. OUTFITTERS	024				840						
"	A.B. DICK CORP.	025				7446						
	SEE	026										
	"	027						123372	134-	449	7628	ø

Chapter 3.
Important Details: Other Areas of Concern

AUTHORIZATION GUIDELINES

In all systems involving the expenditure of funds, someone must have the authority to make purchase commitments for goods and services. When those goods and services have been received, other members of the organization must be in a position of authority to certify receipts and approve payments.

Authorizing Expenditures

In most library situations, the acquisitions librarian authorizes the purchase of books and similar or related materials. Other individuals within the organization may be called upon to authorize expenditures for supplies, equipment, and other goods and services. A second signature from another library official as well as a third signature from the director of central purchasing may be required before the purchase order is issued.

Placing the authorization to make expenditures as close as possible to the various order points (acquisitions, supplies, orders, etc.) not only speeds up the order process, but also relieves other library administrators from the burden of automatically authorizing expenditures without expert knowledge of the details involved in each individual order. The acquisitions librarian, for example, knows the background of the orders being processed and can provide knowledgeable authorization. By the same token, a person charged with the purchase of supplies often is sufficiently familiar with that category of purchases to make sound judgments.

Spelling Out Policy and Procedures

Many libraries don't bother to formalize this sequence of authorization signatures. The procedure is simply understood, for it has been a recognized routine as long as anyone can remember. Nevertheless, a policy spelling out the lines of authority and responsibility is essential to good management. When everyone involved in your purchasing and accounting routines knows who within the organization has the authority to expend funds, the process of acquiring materials and contracting for services becomes much less complicated.

If you rely primarily upon an account clerk to handle the day-to-day operation of your accounting systems, for example, you should identify both the levels and the limits of authority built into that position. In such a case, specify the extent of that individual's authority to make clerical decisions needed to routinely post encumbrances and expenditures as well as to process invoices and credits.

If you already possess a carefully prepared, detailed policy and procedures manual, make sure it contains answers to the obvious routine questions which can arise daily. With the manual identifying levels of authorization as well as ready-made solutions to routine problems, your clerical staff can rely upon policies established in advance by management. Routine clerical authorization can function in areas such as:

- Depositing checks.
- Determining accounts to charge.
- Making bank deposits.
- Making disbursements from petty cash.
- Signing (approving) student time sheets.
- Approving requisitions or vouchers for amounts under a predetermined figure.

Exceptions, not the routine, should require involvement by management. Once again the manual can be designed to convey an understanding of the kinds of situations which require management decisions. Here are some examples:

- Requesting transfers.
- Authorizing guidelines.
- Approving payroll disbursements and hours worked.
- Approving expenditures in excess of a predetermined figure.

Who Else Can Authorize Expenditures?

Nobody likes to learn that a check hasn't been processed or that an order has yet to be mailed simply because an overworked administrator, who demands to see every payment or order before it is placed, has not had time to approve the purchase order, requisition, or voucher. Such situations do exist. They often result in excessive amounts of time wasted by staff who are obliged to hold up order activity while the administrator with the power to approve is attending to other duties. Often, when the administrator leaves town the approval authority goes with him/her, and all activity requiring a signature has to wait for him/her to return. Matters may be further delayed when the approval authority returns to an overflowing in-basket and mentally relegates the order process to a lower priority while other, more pressing matters are resolved first.

If the director of the organization is required to approve requests for expenditures, design your routines to obtain that approval on a regular basis, possibly once a day. In this way the clerical staff will not have to hold important documents indefinitely awaiting the necessary signatures. Identify the backup person who will provide the necessary authorization when the director is absent. As previously mentioned, the authorization function should be as close to the actual point of encumbrance and expenditure as your organization will permit.

Delegating Authority

Delegating authority is not a matter of putting an unpleasant chore off on someone at a lower level of management. If handled properly, it speeds the flow of paperwork so that the whole payment process, in turn, moves faster. Assuming that a better-informed manager makes a better decision, you may even expect the quality of decisions to improve.

Obviously, some levels of authorization cannot be delegated. For example, a rule in some public libraries requires a member of the library board to countersign each fiscal document. This may appear to be an insurmountable obstacle, but there are ways to improve even that situation. One arrangement to reduce or eliminate delays would be for the trustees to appoint a deputy authorized to approve documents in his/her absence. The staff can have all the paperwork prepared in advance for the deputy's signature and can tailor office routines to that schedule. Under this system nobody need wait unnecessarily for authorization.

The director of libraries or head librarian who is required to sign every fiscal document of major importance may be able to arrange to have another administrator do the actual signing and then merely initial the document. This does not detract from the authority of the director; it merely speeds up the process of doing business. Don't neglect the possibility of using a signature stamp to which the authorizing initials can be added. This technique, depending upon the legality of the particular situation, can save you substantial amounts of time. The manager who allows a subordinate to sign important papers must design adequate safeguards to make certain that the signature will not be misused.

What we've arrived at is a series of individual policies or guidelines which may be used for each level of authority. The clerk, who posts records and expends, possesses authorization guidelines clearly identifying responsibilities and limits of authority. The clerk's supervisor has another level of authorization, and so on up the ladder to the senior administrator. Spelling out the limits within each level guarantees effective operation up to the point at which the next level begins. Without such well-defined levels of authority, nobody will be certain who is responsible for what function; the ensuing complications and misunderstandings can involve the whole system.

Authorization Checklist

1. Establish levels of authorization for all key management personnel.
2. Place approval authority at the lowest responsible level of authority.
3. Give others authority to approve in periods of absence.
4. Set up regular signature schedules.
5. Use appropriate devices (stamps, signature machines) to substitute whenever the situation permits.

Allowing for Incompetence

There is another side to the authorization coin. Contrary to the ideal workplace described in management texts, libraries often operate under restrictive personnel programs that do not allow for the ready removal of incompetent persons. In essence, some organizations cannot place responsibility for authorization with the person closest to the activity in question (purchasing, accounting, etc.) if, for some reason, that person does not possess the required judgment and management skills. This need for a higher authorization, which often arises in libraries, requires the involvement of the next highest level of management. Bypassing an inept manager may result in a greater burden for the person who takes on the authorization duties, but it ensures fiscal control and guarantees a certain level of competence in carrying out the fiscal responsibilities of the organization.

CODING

If data processing services are used within the library or by the central business office, the library fiscal documents are probably required to be coded for the computer. Coding may take place in the central business office or in the data processing center. Such coding is usually done in order to assign each fiscal transaction to a specific account. It may also serve to group expenditures by function or area through the use of standard object codes.

The library should be aware of 2 points concerning coding:

- Errors in coding can appear in reports issued by the central accounting office and can often result in commitments or expenditures being made against the wrong account. These errors in coding are the result of one individual assigning a multitude of codes to both library and nonlibrary accounts.

- Business office or data processing center coding can result in delays in payments. If the coding backlog is large and the library must take its turn having fiscal documents coded, delays of several days or weeks often result.

Keep in mind that the more code variations the code clerk must remember or refer to, the greater the opportunity for errors. Fewer errors will occur if only one person handles coding for library goods and services. One way to make coding faster and more reliable is for the library to assume the responsibility for coding its own fiscal documents. If the library can assume this task, there will be:

- Fewer errors, so that funds are not deducted from the wrong account.
- Faster payment to vendors because fiscal documents pass through the system faster.

If a library is permitted to handle its own coding, some expansion of codes may be possible, resulting in the ability of the library to better monitor expenditures. For example, specific codes may be assigned for types of purchases: 580 = books; 610 = periodicals; 410 = cleaning supplies. Under such codes related expenditures may be grouped for easier monitoring.

The staff of any medium-sized library contemplating coding fiscal documents will find that the process is easy to learn and can become a routine procedure. If, however, a library staff has thousands of documents a year to code and could do this coding while preparing requisitions or vouchers, the administrators of that library should consider investing in an electronic typewriter. Such typewriters can be programmed to type the standard codes automatically and follow specific formats, saving a great deal of time for the typist as well as the bookkeeper.

RECONCILING FISCAL REPORTS

An autonomous library which handles all its own financial affairs receives monthly bank statements as a record of routine activity in the library accounts. A library operating as part of a larger organization must rely upon reports from the business office as an indication of what funds have been encumbered or expended officially. This information, whether in the form of bank statements or reports (usually computer printouts) from the business office, serves the same purpose for its respective organizations.

Bank Statements and Computer Printouts

Both forms serve as an official record of expenditure, addition of funds, adjustments, and other transactions. Moreover, both share the same shortcoming of having arrived weeks after the actual activity has taken place, thus leaving the library with a group of current transactions which are not reflected on the official statement or report. If the library relies upon the official record for a balance, while continuing to initiate additional purchases, it runs the risk of over- or underspending. Libraries wishing to expend every dollar without overspending must devise an internal system as previously discussed in order to ensure that encumbrances or expenditures are tied to actual funds available.

The official statement or report should be checked against the internal record of expenditures in the same way that you might compare the transactions listed in your bank statement against the records in your personal check register. The report you receive from the central business office may resemble the printout in figure 22.

Checking for Accuracy

The bank statement or printout the library receives can simply be stamped "received" and filed, since the balance it lists is not the balance indicated in the library records. However, such a procedure is not advisable. Errors do happen—for example, when amounts are deducted from the wrong account or travel expenses are charged to a library book fund. It is a laborious process to check every transaction against your internal records, but discovering incorrect postings can produce substantial savings.

As you check the bank statement or report against internal records, a check mark on both the report and corresponding account records indicates that the charge has been verified. Later, if you receive a statement of your account from a vendor indicating an unpaid invoice, you can easily follow the payment process through your records and prove that the library has faithfully discharged its obligation. The value in having this information at your fingertips should be obvious.

The official statement or report should be checked as soon after receipt as possible. Errors should not be allowed to go uncorrected. Once the report has been reconciled, any errors noted should be listed and described in detail, including a description of how they should be corrected. Copies of financial documents may be required to support the error list. Such a list should be typed and sent to the people responsible for creating the statement. If verification of the error correction is not received, you should be prepared to follow up. Corrections should appear on the following monthly report. If no correction is made, someone within the library, with more authority or clout, should then follow up. Lack of error correction may mean loss of monies for the library.

During the fiscal year, the library may receive additional funds through interest from investments, tax support, special grants, or supplementary allocations. Check your statements or reports to be sure these deposits have been made to the appropriate accounts. Public library systems should also monitor fine deposits.

WRAPPING UP THE FISCAL YEAR

As the end of the fiscal year approaches and your library begins the process of closing its accounts, you normally face one of 2 choices: (1) expending all funds allocated to the library by a certain date, upon penalty of forfeiting the remaining balance at the end of the fiscal year; or (2) carrying over funds into the next fiscal year. Regardless of which alternative you must choose, your manual system will have enabled you to keep tabs on all your encumbrances and expenditures during the past year. Through this system you can compile regular management reports detailing your patterns of expenditure and can monitor all your expenditures. You will now have all the documentation necessary to carry funds into the next fiscal year, if appropriate, and you should also be prepared to make corrections necessary to reconcile your books to show the required end-of-year zero balances in all accounts. Your in-house reporting system is the key to successful budget management.

Identifying the Problem

Why do some libraries spend all their allocations in certain areas, books for example, long before the end of the fiscal year? "We weren't allocated enough money for books this year, so we spent it all in the first couple of months." That familiar complaint would not have to be voiced if the lamenting librarians had a basic system for allocating funds and monitoring their expenditures. It is relatively easy to spread an allocation over an entire fiscal year, no matter how few dollars are involved. Running out of funds before the end of the year usually occurs because there is no clear picture of the status of library accounts. Unless the library has an up-to-the-minute internal accounting system providing daily balances and frequent reporting, it is easy to overspend. If order activity has been high during the year, funds can be drastically overcommitted long before the end of the year.

Why do some libraries suddenly find more money than they can spend before the end of a given fiscal period? How do they get into the situation in the first place?

Twenty years ago, the sudden arrival of a federal grant sent a lot of library administrators into a buying panic. Many of them had no means of monitoring expenditures from the grant and the sudden influx of substantial amounts of money placed a tremendous burden on their order personnel. In many cases librarians

FIGURE 22. Examples of printout reports for books and for supplies.

RUN DATE:11/05/80-17:44:41
PROGRAM : APLDGR

MIAMI UNIVERSITY-OXFORD,OHIO   PAGE 315

DEPARTMENTAL APPROPRIATION LEDGER   OCTOBER 1980

DATE	P.O. NO.	CHECK NO.	DESCRIPTION	PGST REF	ORJ	ALLOTMENTS	DISBURSEMENTS	ENCUMBRANCES	UNENCUMBERED BALANCE
10/21/80	003150	25491	BOSTON UNIVERSITY	DL	586		4.50		
10/21/80	001457	25492	E J BRILL-LONDON	DL	586		36.32		
10/21/80	001438	25494	CRC PRESS INC.	DL	586		58.38		
10/21/80	001439	25497	CHRON GUID PUBL. IN..	DL	586		1.50		
10/21/80	001440	25499	ARTHUR H CLARK CO	DL	586		32.81		
10/21/80	001443	25507	EDUCATIONAL ENRICHMENT	DL	586		113.40		
10/21/80	001444	25514	THEODORE FRONT-MUSIC	DL	586		15.50		
10/21/80	001444	25514	THEODORE FRONT-MUSIC	DL	586		17.00		
10/21/80	001444	25514	THEODORE FRONT-MUSIC	DL	585		115.76		
10/21/80	001471	25515	GENERAL TELEPHONE CO.	DL	586		15.30		
10/21/80	001445	25517	OTTO HARRASSOWITZ	DL	586		205.27		
10/21/80	001446	25519	ROBERT G HAYMAN	DL	586		10.81		
10/21/80	001447	25521	HOLDEN-DAY INC	DL	586		13.68		
10/21/80	001448	25526	INST/FOR SOCIAL RES	DL	586		17.83		
10/21/80	001472	25544	MUSICAL HERITAGE SOC	DL	586		135.75		
10/21/80	001452	25549	W W NORTON & CO INC	DL	586		13.09		
10/21/80	001452	25549	W W NORTON & CO INC	DL	595		17.84		
10/21/80	001453	25550	THE ORYX PRESS	DL	586		13.20		
10/21/80	001454	25551	OXFORD UNIV PRESS	DL	586		39.76		
10/21/80	001455	25554	PHILOSOPHY DOMIN CTR	DL	583		10.73		
10/21/80	001456	25558	PUBLISHERS CENTRAL EUR	DL	586		127.69		
10/21/80	001458	25567	SCHOLARLY BOOK CNTR	DL	586		16.70		
10/21/80	001458	25567	SCHOLARLY BOOK CNTR	DL	586		53.68		
10/21/80	001458	25567	SCHOLARLY BOOK CNTR	DL	586		74.52		
10/21/80	001460	25579	UNIV/WASHINGTON PRESS	DL	586		8.17		
10/21/80	001461	25584	JOHN WILEY & SON INC	DL	586		25.11		
10/24/80	005157	26147	WILLIAM S. HEIN & CO.	DL	586		41.30		
10/24/80	006159	26251	F W FAXON INC	DL	586		346.00		
10/24/80	006162	26381	TREASURER MIAMI UNIV	DL	586		5.00		
10/24/80	006156	26387	UNIVERSAL SERIALS/BOOK	DL	585		2.94		
10/24/80	006156	26387	UNIVERSAL SERIALS/BOOK	DL	586		8.51		
10/24/80	006156	26387	UNIVERSAL SERIALS/BOOK	DL	506		19.65		
10/24/80	006156	26387	UNIVERSAL SERIALS/BOOK	DL	586		75.16		
10/27/80	001549	26578	ARETE PUBLISHING CO.	DL	586		716.00		
10/27/80	001551	26580	ASTOR-HONOR, INC.	DL	586		9.70		
10/27/80	001576	26582	BIBLIOTHEQVE NATIONALE	DL	586		126.59		
10/27/80	001577	26583	THE BRITISH PAPER AND	DL	586		7.21		
10/27/80	001496	26584	PAUL H BROOKES PUBL.	DL	586		17.76		
10/27/80	001497	26586	THE CENTER FOR	DL	586		899.40		
10/27/80	001579	26589	COLUMBIA SPECIAL PROD.	DL	586		46.01		
10/27/80	001500	26590	COMPOSERS RECORDINGS	DL	586		9.28		
10/27/80	001502	26595	EDISON RECORD	DL	586		14.96		
10/27/80	001502	26595	EDISON RECORD	DL	586		103.11		
10/27/80	001503	26596	EDUCATIONAL IMAGES	DL	586		125.08		
10/27/80	001504	26597	EDUCATIONAL SOLUTIONS	DL	586		125.15		
10/27/80	001580	26599	EUROCLASS RECORD DIST-	DL	586		10.98		
10/27/80	001507	26600	FODORS & MCKAY	DL	585		9.31		
10/27/80	001507	26600	FODORS & MCKAY	DL	585		9.90		
10/27/80	001574	26603	INSTITUTE OF NORTIC	DL	586		30.00		
10/27/80	001515	26603	WILLIAM S. HEIN & CO.	DL	586		10.90		
10/27/80	001541	26604	THE HEINEMANN GROUP OF	DL	585		22.54		
10/27/80	001518	26606	IMPACT PRESS, INC.	DL	586		37.73		
10/27/80	001517	26608	INFORMATION FUTURES	DL	586		9.20		

FIGURE 22. Examples of printout reports for books and for supplies. (continued)

```
RUN DATE:11/05/80-17:40:41                    MIAMI UNIVERSITY-OXFORD,OHIO                    PAGE   304
PROGRAM : AFLDGR                        DEPARTMENTAL APPROPRIATION LEDGER        OCTOBER 1980
```

C	DATE	P.C. NO.	CHECK NO.	DESCRIPTION	POST REF	OBJ	ALLOTMENTS	DISBURSEMENTS	ENCUMBRANCES	UNENCUMBERED BALANCE
4C	10/17/80	035324	24598	JM WOODHULL INC	DL	310		22.28	22.28	
4C	10/17/80	035411	94108	JS LATTA INC	DL	310		55.13	45.00	
4P	10/17/80	035413	94154	AMER/PRTN/HUS FR BLIND	DL	310		22.85	22.85	
4P	10/17/80	035413	94154	AMER/PRTN/HUS FR BLIND	DL	310		155.00	155.00	
4C	10/17/80	035503	94226	HATHAWAY STAMP CO	DL	310		429.15	427.30	
4C	10/17/80	035860	94365	NATIONWIDE PAPERS INC	DL	310		710.50	710.50	
4C	10/17/80	035699	94271	OLYMPIA USA INC	DL	310		80.26	81.89	
4C	10/20/80	037008		LEI INC	EJ	310			80.65	
5A	10/20/80			JV 221 BUDG ADJ	EJ	310	810.00			196.09
4	10/21/80	037123	23475	EL-BEE OFFICE OUTFITRS	EJ	310		20.90		
4	10/21/80	000298	25509	AM MULTIGRAPHICS	DL	310		8.56		
4	10/21/80	000310	25518	EL-BEE OFFICE OUTFITRS	DL	310		14.16		
4	10/21/80	000323		HATHAWAY STAMP CO	DL	310				
4	10/21/80	000312	25523	ITT WORLD COMMUNICATN	DL	310		8.58	23.20	
4C	10/21/80	035591	25897	UNIVERSITY PRODUCTS	DL	310		28.60	45.05	
4C	10/23/80	035418	25917	BRODART INC	DL	310		45.05	13.65	
4C	10/23/80	035928		CONSOLIDATED INC	DL	310		13.65		
4P	10/23/80	035730	26003	JM WOODHULL INC	DL	310		70.16	70.16	
4C	10/23/80	035730	26003	JM WOODHULL INC	DL	310		853.31	852.03	
4	10/24/80	000329	26208	CAMERONS OFFICE SP CO	DL	310		56.00		
4	10/24/80	000330	26265	HATHAWAY STAMP CO	DL	310		13.60		
2	10/27/80	037547		GAYLORD BROS INC	EJ	310			110.45	
2	10/27/80	037548		GENERAL LIGHTING PROD	EJ	310			70.80	
2	10/27/80	037560		READEX MICROPRINT CORP	EJ	310			58.00	
4C	10/27/80	035634	26511	THE MAGAFILE CO	DL	310		87.47	93.00	
4C	10/27/80	035463	26517	TALAS	DL	310		6.81	7.38	
4C	10/27/80	035422	26525	CAVALIER AUDIO VISUALS	DL	310		112.50	112.50	
4C	10/27/80	035617	26529	CONSOLIDATED INC	DL	310		289.00	289.00	
4C	10/27/80	035320	26557	OLYMPIA USA INC	DL	310		154.30	157.44	
2	10/29/80	037535		L & I COPERATIVE SRVC	EJ	310			94.05	
2	10/29/80	037586		L & I COOPERATIVE SRVC	EJ	310			318.01	
4P	10/30/80	035124	27211	NATIONWIDE PAPERS INC	DL	310		5.89	5.89	
4P	10/30/80	035860	27211	NATIONWIDE PAPERS INC	DL	310		114.86	131.70	
4C	10/30/80	035124	27211	NATIONWIDE PAPERS INC	DL	310		320.46	326.89	
4C	10/30/80	035725	27225	SPECIALTY ENVELOPE CO	DL	310		124.70	124.70	
31	10/31/80			INTERDEPARTMENTAL CHG	DL	310		47.51		
31	10/31/80			INTERDEPARTMENTAL CHG	DL	310		29.30		
31	10/31/80			INTERDEPARTMENTAL CHG	DL	310		54.35		
31	10/31/80			INTERDEPARTMENTAL CHG	DL	310		287.54		
31	10/31/80			INTERDEPARTMENTAL CHG	DL	310		68.84		
31	10/31/80			INTERDEPARTMENTAL CHG	DL	310		31.32		
4	10/31/80	000342	27389	PORTER ELECTRONICS CO	DL	310		12.10		
4	10/31/80	000361	27511	EL-BEE OFFICE OUTFITRS	DL	310		12.80		
4	10/31/80	000340	27538	HATHAWAY STAMP CO	DL	310		21.41		
4	10/31/80	000300	27640	RADIO SHACK CORP	DL	310		24.95		
7	10/31/80	008407	24484	CANC VO#24484	CL	310		100.70		
4	10/31/80	035771	27227	SWALLEN'S	DL	310		569.81		
4	10/31/80			JV 011 EXP DEC		310		42.50		
4	10/31/80			JV 011 EXP DEC		310		11.00		
4	10/31/80			JV 011 EXP DEC		310		1.00		
4	10/31/80			JV 011 EXP DEC		310		7.50		
4	10/31/80			INTERDEPARTMENTAL CHG		310		77.08		
4	10/31/80			JV 111 MISC		310		40.00		

made large purchases in order to expend substantial amounts of money quickly with minimal effort simply to get rid of the money before the expiration of the grant. Because it was difficult for these libraries to keep track of their money in the first place, they felt more secure expending it in large chunks rather than in many individual transactions which they knew from experience would be difficult to monitor accurately.

The days of the large federal grants are over, but the concept of dealing with large amounts of money, especially near the end of the fiscal year, is far from extinct. Take the example of a large periodicals budget: a lump sum is allocated to cover expenditures for periodicals throughout the fiscal year. In dealing with the allocation, consider such variables as inflation, currency exchange fluctuations, general price increases, and the cost of new subscriptions. Unless expenditures from that allocation are monitored closely during the year, it is entirely possible that by year end the periodicals allocation could be seriously over- or underspent— in either case, an undesirable situation.

The real culprit is a lack of planning. If a spending program had been worked out in anticipation of all the factors mentioned above, the orderly expenditure of the allocation could begin the minute the funds were received. It is possible to plan in advance, work out all the purchasing arrangements ahead of time, and even set up a separate group of accounts in which to record commitments.

Planning for the End of the Year

With an orderly internal accounting system providing up-to-date statistics, you will be able to tell early in the fiscal year which accounts are not being expended at the prescribed rate. You will be able to identify surplus funds and make sure that those responsible for expending them have plenty of advance warning.

What if your internal accounting system is "unofficial," however, and exists merely as a device to monitor expenditures and encumbrances and control the disbursement of your allocations? What if you approach the end of the fiscal year with a number of orders encumbered on your internal records but not encumbered on the "official" organization's books? This often happens in university systems where the library issues purchase orders to vendors but does not encumber those orders in the central accounting records. There may well be a $100,000 free balance shown on the official central accounting books, but the library records reveal that every bit of that $100,000 has been encumbered internally among a variety of vendors. If

the books, periodicals, and supplies representing the $100,000 are not received and paid for by the end of the fiscal year, the library will have to forfeit the $100,000 and pay for the items in the next fiscal year, creating a further problem for librarians and library administrators.

Examples of several methods of holding funds beyond the end of the fiscal year are discussed below. The objective in all cases is to find means of preserving the funds in order to pay for goods and services committed during the fiscal year in question. This list of methods is far from complete; other ways to accomplish the same thing vary from organization to organization.

Simple Carry Forward. In libraries where the internal accounting system is the only system, it is a simple matter to carry the money forward into the next fiscal year. Many large public libraries have this ability and retaining funds from one year to the next is a routine matter accomplished by the library business office.

Various Vendors Purchase Order. Depending upon the policies governing your institution's central accounting system, it might be possible to formally encumber all your outstanding internal library purchase orders on one, official, institutional purchase order (see figure 23). The actual purchase order becomes nothing more than an encumbering document with no vendor indicated. The document is supported by photocopies of pages from your internal accounting ledger, which bears the library order number, the name of the vendor, the fund, the amount, and the date ordered. On the ledger page, place checks or stars by each item which is reflected on this particular purchase order. Make certain they all add up to the total amount on the face of the purchase order. Acting upon the authority of this official purchase order, the accounting department records the encumbrance total and the purchase order number and thus effectively holds or reserves the funds from the current fiscal year into the next. Depending upon the institution's policies, that money may be held until every individual library purchase order has been paid. The official purchase order itself is not mailed.

Single Vendor Purchase Order. If a substantial number of orders are outstanding with one vendor, it may be possible to issue a blanket purchase order in that vendor's name (see figure 24) and to support it, once again, by attaching to it photocopies of pages from your internal accounting ledger showing the library order number, the name of the vendor, the fund, the amount, and the date ordered. Again, simply check or star the items in your ledger which pertain to this purchase order. Make certain they add up to the total amount on the face of the purchase order. Because the library purchase orders have already been issued, the blanket

FIGURE 23. Example of a blanket purchase order for various vendors.

FIGURE 24. Example of a single vendor blanket purchase order.

PURCHASE ORDER	MIAMI UNIVERSITY		P. O. NO. 44099
	PURCHASING OFFICE • OXFORD, OHIO 45056		ALL INVOICES, PACKAGES, PACKING SLIPS, DELIVERY TICKETS, MUST SHOW THIS NUMBER.
	Telephone (513) 529-2125		

			DEPT. REQUISITION NO. LIB L-3789	MONTH 6	P.O. DATE DAY 01	YEAR 80

STATE AGENCY 285

F.O.B.	DELIVERY PROMISED	YOUR QUOTE NO. AND DATE	TERMS

☐ MIAMI UNIVERSITY   ☐ Days ☐ Weeks ☐ At Once

MATERIAL ON THIS ORDER IS EXEMPT FROM PAYMENT OF THE OHIO SALES TAX SEC. 2-1 A.M. H.B- NO. 134 AND ALL FED. TAX.

T O

Famous Bookseller
GPO P.O. 555
Somerwell, N.Y.

MAIL ALL INVOICES TO:
MIAMI UNIVERSITY
PURCHASING OFFICE
213 ROUDEBUSH HALL
OXFORD, OHIO 45056

SHIP TO: (UNLESS OTHERWISE INDICATED BELOW)
MIAMI UNIVERSITY
CENTRAL RECEIVING
COLE SERVICE BLDG.
OXFORD, OHIO 45056

MIAMI UNIVERSITY IS AN EQUAL OPPORTUNITY EMPLOYER

QUANTITY	UNIT	DESCRIPTION AND/OR SPECIFICATION	UNIT PRICE	AMOUNT
		Blanket encumbrance for Library Book orders indicated by circles on attached xerox pages of library order records		$89,900

DIRECT ALL QUESTIONS TO:

NOTICE TO SUPPLIER:

1. SEND INVOICES IN DUPLICATE ON YOUR OWN INVOICE FORMS.
2. SHOW CASH DISCOUNT TO WHICH MIAMI UNIVERSITY IS ENTITLED ON YOUR INVOICE.
3. PLEASE ACKNOWLEDGE RECEIPT OF THIS ORDER AND GIVE SHIPPING DATE.
4. ALL GOODS ORDERED AND RECEIVED ARE SUBJECT TO TEST AND INSPECTION, AND IF REJECTED SHALL REMAIN THE PROPERTY OF THE VENDOR.
5. ALL INVOICES MUST SHOW THE VENDOR'S FEDERAL TAX NUMBER.
6. PLEASE SHOW MANUFACTURER'S SERIAL NUMBER ON INVOICE FOR EACH OF THE ABOVE ITEMS HAVING A SERIAL NUMBER. IF THIS NUMBER IS NOT SHOWN PAYMENT WILL BE WITHHELD.

BUYER

BY _____
DIRECTOR OF PURCHASES

MU-6054

purchase order vendor copy is not mailed. The blanket purchase order follows the same supporting documentation role played by the various vendors purchase order. The accounting copy is held along with the marked photocopies of the library accounting ledger pages attached to it and, as invoices are presented, they are deducted from the total encumbrance.

Blanket Encumbrance. If the financial structure of the institution or library permits establishing a formal encumbrance for each library allocation at the beginning of the fiscal year, the funds can then be held indefinitely until there arc cnough invoices submitted for payment to exhaust the encumbrance. This method has the advantage of virtually eliminating the end-of-year worries over spending every penny, because in effect it ties up the funds for the exclusive use of the library. On the negative side, however, it violates the fiscal-year concept to spend 1981 funds in 1981 and actually allows monies budgeted for one fiscal year to be committed and expended in the next. Libraries employing this method often produce confusing budget reports which contain both "old" and "new" money. Figure 25 shows how a blanket encumbrance may be used as a fiscal document against which payments are charged. The blanket encumbrance is similar to a blanket purchase order in that it retains funds for the library to use for future purchases.

Ethics and Good Working Relations

Finding ways to retain the use of funds from one year to the next should not be a problem as long as the funds in question represent actual commitments (orders) made during the fiscal year in question. If you give a vendor an order, you have committed your organization to a payment upon receipt of the goods. If the goods arrive after the end of the fiscal year your obligation to pay has not diminished. Therefore, from an ethical standpoint, you do have a claim to the funds you have obligated. By using various vendors or blanket purchase orders, you are merely establishing your claim to the previous year's funds, funds you were unable to formally expend through no fault of your own.

An appeal to carry over funds from one year to the next because you simply neglected to commit them is a completely different situation, which will receive little sympathy. Most accounting and purchasing people can easily understand the vagaries of the marketplace and readily acknowledge delays, which can exceed normal delivery schedules. They realize that your library book order form represents a legal commitment to purchase. What many of them would not readily concede is your

right to retain until spent those funds you have not committed during the normal course of your budget year.

If it is difficult to convince a reluctant purchasing agent or comptroller that your purchasing needs are unique or at least substantially different from those of your parent organization, make an effort to bring him/her to your office for an orientation. S/he may need to become familiar with your particular purchasing and accounting problems; upon knowing the kinds of difficulties you face, s/he will be in a much better frame of mind when approached with potential solutions. Keeping all interested parties informed and aware of what is going on can produce tangible benefits when it is necessary to seek assistance.

FOLLOW-UP WITH RELUCTANT VENDORS

In many if not most institutions, materials ordered must be received before an invoice may be approved for payment. Once you have received the goods or services ordered, you are obligated to process the invoice for payment promptly. The vendor has lived up to his/her promise to deliver and, unless there is a justifiable reason to hold up the payment process, s/he expects to receive payment in full. Prompt payment helps make your business relationship with your vendor a good one. Many vendors have learned to expect prompt payment only if they send an invoice with each shipment. Thus, on sheet invoices (where numbers of individual items are listed) payment is initiated only when all items have been received.

Separate Invoicing by Shipment

To give the vendor an opportunity to receive regular payments from the library while reducing the need for internal paperwork within the library, librarians should insist that all shipments be invoiced separately. When vendors adhere to this policy they can expect prompt payment, since shipments with invoices normally require a minimum of processing on the part of the library. Some exceptions can arise in which the vendor may demand payment even though the library has yet to receive the goods. Cash flow, or the balance between income and expenditure, is of particular concern to vendors. It involves the step-by-step tracing of the vendor's income from the time it arrives in the form of a customer's payment until it goes out in the form of a payroll check or a payment for inventory. Detailed cash

FIGURE 25. Blanket encumbrance.

Library Books • Periodicals • Binding
Library Name

Library Encumbrance Number

Date _____   _____

☐ Library Books   ☐ Library Supplies

☐ Library Periodicals   ☐ Library Equipment

☐ Library Binding   ☐ Other

Fund Name

Fund Number
Amount to Encumber $ _____

Items Received   Balance

flow statements are used to predict future profits, assess current borrowing needs, and even forecast corporate growth. The cash flow statement is seen as a yardstick for measuring the firm's degree of success in attaining company goals.

Collecting payments in sufficient amounts on a regular, predictable schedule permits the vendor to make regular expenditures for business expenses such as personnel, supplies, and inventory, without the need to borrow money. If a company is not able to maintain a favorable cash flow, it must borrow money to keep the organization functioning until the customers pay their obligations. In today's tight money market, a vendor who does not receive payment within a certain time period, usually 30 to 90 days, faces the prospect of borrowing money. To avoid high interest rates and the extra costs that go with short-term borrowing, vendors will first attempt to collect through the old, reliable techniques of generating frequent customer statements, making dunning phone calls, and sending letters demanding payment. All are intended to gather cash by reminding the delinquent customer of overdue invoices.

What many libraries must realize, however, is that some vendors may be more interested in resolving their immediate cash flow problems than in making sure that all order obligations have been fulfilled. It is vital that the library follow up immediately when the vendor fails to meet delivery obligations. If the follow-up is carried out when the problem first occurs, the incident is fresh in everybody's mind. After several months of waiting, the incident will be difficult to recall and even more difficult to resolve.

After all the invoices have been approved, most libraries are capable of paying promptly. Some libraries, however, are slow to pay. This tardiness is often caused by reliance upon a nonlibrary organization (the accounting department of a large university, for example). Even though the library has presented approved invoices for payment promptly, it often finds that they were held in accounting for several weeks before checks were written and mailed.

Checking Statements

If your internal accounting system includes routine procedures for checking those potential problem statements as soon as they arrive, you'll know exactly what your obligations are and will not only be able to correct any errors your system has produced but also be in an excellent position to respond quickly and accurately to any questions the statements pose about the status of your account. Too many libraries ignore the vendor's statement. "They know we always pay our bills" is a frequent library response. Vendors may view you as a responsible customer, but if you don't pay strict attention to what's contained in a particular series of statements, you may be in for a surprise when you suddenly find an angry vendor on your doorstep.

This doesn't mean you'll want to check every customer statement you receive. If you institute a regular routine of spot checking, the clerk to whom you assign this task will soon learn which customer statements require special attention. An experienced statement checker needs only to glance at a statement to know whether something out of the ordinary requires careful analysis. Experience teaches you how to select those statements which are potential problems. For example, some statements, because of the reliability of the vendor and the high level of accuracy and detail involved in all your business transactions, will need no more than a casual glance. Other statements produced by vendors with whom you have had numerous difficulties will need to be checked carefully, item by item, to make sure that every item listed agrees with your records. You will learn through experience which vendors tend to list invoices on statements before you could possibly receive the goods. The account clerk or other person assigned to check statements and follow up on potential problems will be in the enviable position of being on top of current order/payment activity and able to resolve difficulties while they are still minor ones.

When checking statements, ask yourself these questions:

1. Is the address on the statement correct? If not, this is a good time to request a change.
2. Is the account number on the vendor's statement yours? Account numbers can get switched, resulting in one library being dunned for another library's overdue account.
3. Is each of the invoices listed yours?
4. Does the statement reflect items the library ordered, not goods ordered by another department within the parent organization?
5. Is the amount correct?
6. Do your receiving records support the invoice?
7. Was the check actually issued?
8. Has your check had time to reach the vendor?

Don't assume the problem statement you receive indicates an error for which you are responsible. The accounts receivable department of many of the larger vendors may not be aware that their order fulfillment department has failed to ship all of the items reflected by the invoices listed on the customer statement. By checking the statement, your account clerk can trace the lack of payment to orders that have not yet been received. Depending upon the degree to which the vendor is pressing for payment, the acquisitions librarian or persons responsible for expending the funds may return the statement to the vendor with a form letter noting the error, or may simply discard the statement, assuming that the items will be received and payment processed before the next statement appears. If a second statement arrives indicating the same problems, contact the vendor immediately.

REFUNDS

Occasionally, a vendor refunds a payment. Rather than appearing in the form of a credit memo, the refund or credit may be a check. Ideally, the funds represented by the check should find their way back into the library account from which they were expended. However, in some institutions, policy requires that all refunds be deposited into a central account; thus, a refund check directed to the library would not appear as a credit to a library account. The money it represents would, in effect, be lost to the library.

Receiving Proper Credits

Whenever possible, refund checks should be used to replenish the account from which they were originally drawn. If checks are not allowed to be deposited as a general credit, they may be deposited as a credit against the expenditures already made from a given account. Thus a $50 refund check may be deposited in order to ''decrease the expenditures in library account 'X' by $50.'' If this refund is related to one or more internal library funds, those funds should receive proper credit on the internal books as well.

Check Transmittal Forms

When many refunds and check cancellations are processed each year, a check transmittal form may be used (see figure 26). Such a form should indicate clearly and consistently how monies are to be deposited or credited. The same mechanism may be used to deposit cash through a central business office.

FIGURE 26. Check transmittal form.

Transmittal Form
Library Name

To: _____

From: _____   Date _____

Please process the attached receipt(s):

I. Activity
   ☐ Cancel and Credit
   ☐ Decrease Expenditures

II. Account Involved
   ☐ Library-Books
      0-2-0-003-21-20-586
   ☐ Library-Standing Orders
      0-2-0-003-21-20-587
   ☐ Library-Periodicals
      0-2-0-003-21-20-510
   ☐ Library-Other Expense-Supplies
      0-2-0-003-21-20-310
   ☐ Library-Other Expense-Interlibrary Loan
      0-2-0-003-21-20-560
   ☐ Library-Postage
      0-2-0-003-21-20-570
   ☐ Newsletter-Deposit #9022
   ☐ Other

Total Cash Enclosed _____

\#_____Cks
   Totaling _____

TOTAL _____

Cash and Checks Represent: _____

_____

_____

If there is a question, call (account clerk name and extension number).

FOR LIBRARY USE ONLY

Credit Internal Fund _____
cc: Library Account Clerk

Chapter 4.
Those Other Accounts You Have to Manage

TAXES, POSTAGE, SHIPPING, AND HANDLING CHARGES

A variety of additional charges usually appears at the bottom of invoices. Postage, shipping, and handling charges are acceptable. Taxes, however, depending upon your library's tax status, may constitute an improper charge.

Taxes

If your library is a tax-exempt organization, you may be asked to prove this status so that your library is not automatically taxed for goods purchased. To avoid any misunderstandings, you may also want to display your tax I.D. number on all orders. You may wish to refer to USCA 26, Section 501, the tax-exempt citation. Publication 557, *How to Apply for and Retain Exempt Status for Your Organization,* describes the procedures through which an organization may obtain tax-exempt status. It is available from the Department of the Treasury, Internal Revenue Service.

It is important that all individuals checking your invoices be aware of your tax status so that any taxes which appear can be deducted. If a vendor questions such a deduction, be prepared to supply your I.D. number and cite the law if necessary.

Postage, Shipping, and Handling Charges

The other miscellaneous charges that can be levied on invoices are not so easily ignored. Some libraries maintain separate postage and shipping accounts to accommodate these charges. This method provides a total picture of the charges paid during any fiscal year, but under this arrangement the funds responsible for these charges are not paying them. A more acceptable method is to charge back to the separate funds any postage, shipping, or handling fees incurred.

Equipment and supply purchases which incur shipping charges may be dealt with by apportioning the charges among the items ordered. The shipping charges which appear on sheet invoices for books and periodicals are more difficult to deal with. They may list dozens or even hundreds of items with the total shipping or handling charge appearing at the end of the invoice. This charge may be paid on a separate fund; however, it is more equitable to levy such charges against the actual funds on which the materials were originally ordered. This can be done in one of 2 ways.

- Choose one book or periodical at random and pay all the charges on the fund from which that book or periodical was ordered. If the charge is a small one, this random selection method is the simplest to follow. By the end of the fiscal year, all funds will end up having been tapped for these charges.
- Divide the charges equally among all the funds involved. This method is recommended if the charges are substantial, as might be the case with a periodical invoice or a very large book shipment.

Look for Exceptions

Finally, if your contract with the vendor states that you are not to be charged for shipping or handling, be prepared to remind the vendor of the agreement should such charges appear on the invoice. It is equally important for the clerk handling these particular invoices to understand the special invoicing arrangements and question any shipping or handling charges which may appear.

MANAGING CASH

At some point someone in most organizations must deal with cash. Collecting fines and payments for overdue, lost, or stolen books is one area in which handling cash is necessary. If the library has branches at which cash collections are made, the magnitude of the problem is increased. The procedure of managing cash collections for a multibranch operation remains the same as for a single library but, because more people are involved, this process can be frustrating. Although making the routines simple and the paperwork minimal helps, complications nevertheless arise due to varying staff interpretations of the procedures.

Making change at the circulation desk in a large public or academic library can require the accounting and control of fairly substantial amounts of cash, usually in small bills and change. In large libraries, with vending machines dispensing everything from soft drinks to photocopies, the demand for change can assume staggering proportions. If the vending machine owner does not provide mechanical change-making equipment, the library must supply hundreds of dollars in nickels, dimes, and quarters each week. Collecting, housing, depositing, distributing, and accounting for large amounts of cash can present a number of special problems for the unwary as well as a predictable number of frustrations for the knowledgeable manager.

Establishing and Housing a Cash Fund

For the purpose of discussion, a hypothetical cash fund of $500.00 is to be used for making change. Assuming the library does not have the ability to issue a check for cash, we start with a requisition or voucher made out to an appropriate library account, such as "Supplies—Miscellaneous." The central accounting office draws a check, debits the library account, and delivers the check to the person authorized by the library to maintain control over the cash fund. If the check is made out in the name of an individual, his/her signature acknowledges receipt for the library.

Cash is a tempting commodity and as such must be treated carefully. It must be protected from impromptu withdrawals by unauthorized individuals and yet be readily available for its intended use. Minimal security for any cash fund, no matter how small, is a locked cash drawer. Under no circumstances should you consider keeping cash in any container (such as a metal box) which is even remotely portable. If it can be physically removed from the premises, assume that it will be, and find another container.

A combination safe is the best solution to the cash security problem. Make certain you find one that is reasonably secure, and has appropriate fire underwriter's approval; then locate it away from the public view. Keep it locked at all times and restrict the combination to the person or persons needing access.

Responsibility for a Cash Fund

The person who signs a check or other instrument initiating the cash fund is ultimately responsible for the fund. However, s/he may not be the same person who operates the cash fund on a day-to-day basis. Beginning with the original deposit of money into the fund, the cash passes through many hands within the organization. Consequently, all means to assure its control at every step along the line must be carefully worked out. For example, if your account clerk is assigned the responsibility for the safe, make certain that the responsibility is recognized in writing with a formal statement indicating the date and amount on hand and signed by both the account clerk and a witness (see figure 27). If cash is taken from the safe to support a change fund in the circulation department, make certain that it is formally signed out (see figure 28). Keep the completed form with your cash fund. When you are audited, this record not only explains the missing cash but shows that you have taken the proper steps to maintain control over the funds by documenting your actions.

If you do not have a safe and yet must keep cash on the premises, make certain that your cash on hand never exceeds the amount necessary for the routine operation of the library unit. This requires periodic deposits of excess money either to a central library collection point where security is not a problem (see figure 29) or to a branch bank at which an account has been established for this purpose (see figure 30). The night deposit box at the branch bank is an easy means of depositing cash securely. To protect the money which stays in the library, keep your library cash in a locked drawer in an area that is lit at night and, if possible, visible from outside the building. In recent years, branch libraries have increasingly become targets for vandalism and petty thievery. Making the location of the cash box easily viewed at any time of the night discourages many would-be thieves.

Periodic Audits

Depending upon how your cash fund is used, you may need to determine the cash balance at the end of each day. The amount on hand should be logged, dated,

FIGURE 27. Library-vault deposit record.

Vault Deposit Record

Library Name

To: _____

I hereby acknowledge receipt of $ _____

representing _____

_____

_____

_____

Date _____   Received by _____

Witnessed by _____

FIGURE 28. Form to sign out funds.

To: _____

The following cash funds have been transferred to _____

_____

PURPOSE	AMOUNT

Received by _____   Date _____

I certify that the amounts listed above are correct.

_____   _____

Signature   Date

FIGURE 29. Example of a cash-deposit report.   **FIGURE 30. Example of a bank-deposit breakdown.**

Cash Deposit Report	
Date	————————
Agency	————————
Fines	————
Material lost & paid for (send cash received record to overdues)	————
Film fees	————
Film Catalog	————
Bags	————
Miscellaneous	————
Total receipts	════
Less refunds (attach receipt)	————
Cash with deposit	════
Report made by	
————————————	

Send original to Business Office.
Retain duplicate.

Room Rent	$ ————
Telephone Commission	————
Vending Machine Commissions	————
Fines & Desk Receipts	
Branches	————
Main	———— ————
Library Material Lost & Paid	
Branches	————
Main	———— ————
Film Catalog	————
Book Catalog	————
Service Charges	————
Total	$ ════
Received from	————————
Received by	————————
Date	————————

and signed by the person responsible for operating the fund (see figure 31). Even though you balance your cash fund daily and feel secure that everything is being handled properly, you should institute periodic internal audits so you can:

1. Be reassured that your cash fund is in order and all monies are accounted for.

2. Give your clerical staff frequent experience with audits so they will be able to deal effectively with internal and external audits when they occur.

FIGURE 31. Cash fund audit form.

3. Keep a close watch on this most easily misused portion of your fiscal structure.

4. Prevent shortages which have a way of developing in the best managed systems. The more control you exercise with your cash fund, the less likely you are to experience shortages. If you have any second thoughts about the effectiveness of your internal controls, invite your internal auditor to check out your system and advise you on additional techniques to establish more effective controls.

An auditor is unlikely to be available to make frequent spot checks on your cash funds. You'll have to find ways of carrying out that responsibility yourself. If you work out the procedures for cash auditing with the person responsible for handling cash, you will be able to secure that individual's trust and cooperation. Depending upon your organization, its size, and level of staffing, these cash audits may be conducted by a supervisor or another clerk. As long as the cash auditor has the freedom to make random audits, conducts them in the presence of the person responsible for the cash, and then produces a report of the findings signed by both parties, the audit requirement will have been fulfilled. Your need to know that cash is being handled carefully and correctly has been satisfied and your cash clerk has not been placed in a threatening situation because s/he has been involved from the beginning in setting up the actual audit routines.

The audit report need be nothing more than a simple typewritten statement stating the cash balances, including any amounts over or short, and signed by the cash clerk and the auditor.

Receipts and Disbursements

Cash transactions present a number of problems beyond basic security. In most cases, however, it comes down to a need to account for all cash receipts (collections such as fines, payments for lost books, photocopy and vending machine receipts) and cash disbursements (payments, postage stamps, first aid supplies, cleaning supplies, and miscellaneous items) for which a formal check would not be convenient (see figure 32).

In each instance, a receipt or other dated record supporting the transaction must be preserved. If you collect fines or make other collections, you need to enter all your receipts in a record similar to that in figure 33. Copies of the actual receipts must be kept with the cash receipt book to support the entries.

FIGURE 32. Cash collection form.

Cash Collection Sheet		
Library Name _____		
Date	Amount	Name

FIGURE 33. Daily cash report form.

Daily Cash Report
Library Name

Branch _____

Date _____   Reset Number _____

Ending Reading	
Beginning Reading	
Subtotal	
(−) Voids	
Subtotal	
(−) Refunds	
Adjusted Register Total	
Cash Count	
(+) Refunds	
TOTAL	$

Fines & Desk Receipts*	
Library Materials Lost & Paid	
Film Fees	
Bags	
Service Charge	
Film Catalog	
Tax	
Miscellaneous	
Subtotal	
Patron's Deposits (Refund Portion)	
TOTAL	$

For Office Use Only		
	Tax	
	TOTAL	$

Short $ _____

Overage $ _____

Total Number Customers _____

Number of Sales _____

Paid Out $ _____

Voids: attach cash register receipt voided and initialed

Refunds: include receipts of all funds paid out

Report Completed by: _____

_____

_____

_____

*Fines & desk receipts include damages, reserves, nonrefundable portions of deposit cards, paid cards.

Cash Register

For any library in which collections constitute a substantial portion of circulation activity, a cash register is an excellent way to establish control. Such equipment can maintain continuous tapes coded to identify transactions by type. They can even generate a printed receipt bearing the name of your library, the date, and the amount of the transaction, eliminating the need for a time-consuming, hand-written equivalent.

2 JAN81   0998   E *10.50

MIAMI UNIVERSITY LIBRARIES
CIRCULATION SERVICES
KEEP THIS RECEIPT

If you don't have a cash register, you still have an obligation to document each transaction and at the same time provide a receipt for payments. Any number of commercial receipt forms are available for this purpose. They can be prenumbered, printed with your library name, and made available in sets with the required number of copies to support your particular system (see figure 34).

Transporting Funds

If you have to transport your funds to and/or from a bank and you don't have a reasonably safe way to make the transfer, get some advice before you attempt to handle it on your own. Your bank, local police, parent organization, or institutional security force can help you work out a reasonably safe, effective routine.

Whatever plan of action you adopt, make sure you follow a few basic rules designed to reduce the risk of robbery or accidental loss:

1. Keep a low profile. Don't advertise the fact that your courier is carrying money.
2. If you have police protection to and from the bank, don't allow your courier to be out of the officer's sight at any point between the drive to the bank and the return to your building.
3. Keep your bank trips as far away from routine schedules as possible.
4. Provide secure cash bags, especially for heavy change.

Centralizing the Handling of Cash

If your library operation is sufficiently large to justify a centralized cashier's office, you may want to consider such a move as a means of simplifying your cash-handling routines. By establishing a central point in your library where all cash transactions take place, and accounts are kept, you automatically reduce the number of individuals involved in handling cash, improve accuracy, ensure better control and security, and simplify the auditing requirement (see figure 35). One such central cashier's office in a large university library handles all cash collections and payments, provides vault security for a variety of cash funds, and even handles the disbursement of paychecks for library faculty, staff, and students. The cashier's office also issues a receipt indicating the monies received (see figure 36).

TIME SHEETS AND PAYROLL CARDS

To the uninitiated, payroll recordkeeping may appear to be a formidable undertaking. In reality it is no more complicated than any other routine accounting task. As long as there are well-designed routines and procedures to follow, there will be few problems.

In order to compensate employees for their labor, there must be an official record of the time worked. That record must be certified or approved by someone in authority before payment may be made. The categories of payroll records range from the salaried library employee, who is paid by the month and for whom few or no formal record of hours or days worked is kept, all the way to the hourly employee who must certify hours worked by entering them on a time-clock card. The clock card must be approved by a supervisor, whose signature supports the employee's claim. There are many levels of payroll records inbetween, but all have in common the need to support the hours worked with a document that will satisfy an audit.

Payroll Verification

Even though the payroll function in your library may be handled by an outside firm or a central office beyond your jurisdiction, there is usually a certain amount of accounting activity at the local level which must be dealt with at the end of each payroll period. Someone must verify the hours on the time sheets or payroll cards, collect and account for them before they are presented for check preparation, and be prepared to

FIGURE 34. Receipt form.

Receipt for Payment

Library Name

Received from _____

First name   Last name

_____

Address

_____

For material charged to _____

By _____

$ _____   Date _____

Total amount

Payment received for following items	Received for material	Received for fines

Refund for the amount paid for material will be made upon presentation of material AND receipt to an agency of the Library within six months of receipt date. There is *no refund* for payment of fines. *Keep this receipt six months!*

FIGURE 35. Form for transferring cash to central cashier.

Cash Transmittal Form
Library Name

To: _____   Date _____

From: _____

Description (list checks separately)	Amount

Received by _____   Date _____

FIGURE 36. Receipt of money by cashier's office.

		Cashier's Office Library Name		
Received from _____			Number _____	
_____			Date _____	
☐ Library Fines	$_____		☐ Deposits	$_____
☐ Replacements	$_____		☐ Others (describe)	$_____
☐ Coin-operated Copiers	$_____		_____	
Cash	_____		_____	
Checks	_____			
Total	$_____		Initials _____	

distribute the checks which the time sheets ultimately produce.

Clock Cards

Probably the best method for recording time automatically is with the time clock (see figure 37). The time clock is set to print on the employees' cards the time and date in columns arranged by day. Unless the clock malfunctions, the cards present an accurate record of the hours, and fractions thereof, worked by each employee. The individual's name and social security number should appear on each card.

Each completed clock card is verified by a supervisor, whose signature indicates approval of the hours worked. Changes or corrections are made by the supervisor and initialed.

The account clerk may be expected to:

1. Collect the cards according to a prearranged schedule.
2. Check each against a master list of employees.
3. Check for the supervisor's approval signature.
4. Add up the hours worked to make certain they agree with the totals.

Time Sheets

In addition to, or instead of, the time clock, you may have time sheets that are completed manually. Here the margin for error is greater. A supervisor must

still approve each time sheet. The account clerk must either make a more thorough analysis of the hours listed on each sheet, checking arithmetic and days worked, or, if the system permits, take the supervisor's approval literally and forget about checking each time sheet in detail. The time sheet differs from the clock card primarily in that the clock card furnishes a mechanically produced record of the hours worked. The success of the time sheet depends to a great extent upon the willingness of the employees to state their hours accurately and the ability of their supervisors to confirm the hours recorded.

The account clerk may be expected to:

1. Collect the time sheets according to a predetermined schedule.
2. Check each sheet against a master list of employees.
3. Check for necessary approval signature as well as the employee's own signature.
4. Make sure total hours claimed are within the payroll guidelines and, if overtime is indicated, look for supporting authorization.
5. Check computations on time sheet and make any corrections necessary.

Figures 38, 39, and 40 present examples of time sheets and recap sheets for supervisors that can be adapted for use in your library. Each is designed to fit a specific type of payroll, either on a biweekly or monthly payment schedule.

FIGURE 37. Sample time-clock card.

Front	Back
COST CARD	ABSENCES
BUILDING SERV 11/29/80	Date _____ Hours _____
DATE _____	Reason _____

(The figure shows a two-part time-clock card. The front is labeled "COST CARD" with "BUILDING SERV 11/29/80" and a DATE field, with the note "Record Absences and Overtime on the Reverse Side of Card." It has columns headed CLOCK RECORD, Elapsed Time, and JOB No. The clock record shows:

W 16:00
W 11:98
W 11:00

At the bottom:
TOTAL REG. TIME HRS. _____ @ _____
TOTAL OVERTIME HRS. _____ @ _____
TOTAL LABOR COST _____

The back is labeled "ABSENCES" with three blocks each containing Date _____ Hours _____ and Reason _____ lines, then "OVERTIME" with three similar blocks, and finally:
Approved By:
_____
(Supervisor))

FIGURE 38. Example of an individual biweekly time sheet.

Department or Branch _____

Employee _____   Pay Period _____

Indicate actual beginning and quitting time to the nearest 5 minutes

	MORNING		AFTERNOON		EVENING		TOTAL HOURS	Time Lost through Illness	Over-time	Under-time	Vaca-tion	Paid Over-time	REMARKS
	Enter	Leave	Enter	Leave	Enter	Leave							
Sun													
Mon													
Tue													
Wed													
Thu													
Fri													
Sat													
Net Total for Week:													
Sun													
Mon													
Tue													
Wed													
Thu													
Fri													
Sat													
Net Total for Week:													
TOTAL FOR PERIOD:													

I certify the above record is correct.   I certify that the above is correct.

_____   _____
Supervisor   Employee

FIGURE 39. Example of a monthly time sheet for an individual.

Employee _____   Month and Year _____

Date	IN	OUT	IN	OUT	HOURS	LOST TIME	EARNED TIME	NOTES
1								
2								
3								
4								
5								
6								
7								
8								
9								
10								
11								
12								
13								
14								
15								
16								
17								
18								
19								
20								
21								
22								
23								
24								
25								
26								
27								
28								
29								
30								
31								

Sick leave used _____   Vacation used _____

Personal leave used _____   Compensatory used _____

Supervisor _____   Employee _____

Date _____   Date _____

FIGURE 40. Example of supervisor's recap sheet- biweekly time report.

Name		Week beginning, Sunday_____19____								Week beginning, Sunday_____19____							
		Sun	Mon	Tue	Wed	Thu	Fri	Sat	Total Hours	Sun	Mon	Tue	Wed	Thu	Fri	Sat	Total Hours
	Morn																
	Aft																
	Eve																
	Morn																
	Aft																
	Eve																
	Morn																
	Aft																
	Eve																
	Morn																
	Aft																
	Eve																
	Morn																
	Aft																
	Eve																
	Morn																
	Aft																
	Eve																
	Morn																
	Aft																
	Eve																
	Morn																
	Aft																
	Eve																
	Morn																
	Aft																
	Eve																

Approved _____ Department _____
Supervisor

Explanation.   ✓: On duty.   Ill: Illness.   Vac: Vacation.   Dock: Leave without pay.   Abs: Time to be made up.

Along with time sheets and payroll cards, the account clerk may be required to keep a running total of hours worked, vacation and sick leave taken, and leave without pay (see figure 41). In addition, the check stub accompanying the paycheck may indicate cumulated time (see figure 42).

FIGURE 41. Annual payroll summary record.

Title _____	Department _____
Name _____ 19 ___	Date Employed _____

Leave carried forward from 19 _____	V allowance _____	TIME TAKEN			Comp or Hol
V _____	S allowance _____				
S _____	Hol allowance _____				

Month	1	2	3	4	5	6	7	8	9	10	11	12	13	14	15	16	17	18	19	20	21	22	23	24	25	26	27	28	29	30	31	V	S	L	Date
Jan																																			
Feb																																			
Mar																																			
Apr																																			
May																																			
June																																			
July																																			
Aug																																			
Sept																																			
Oct																																			
Nov																																			
Dec																																			
Totals																																			

Leave carried	V _____	V-vacation	C-comp	J-jury duty	D-death in family
forward to 19 _____	S _____	S-sick leave	H-holiday	L-LWOP	M-meeting

FIGURE 42. Example of paycheck stub recapping employees payroll activities.

Earnings			Time Record Accumulation			
Earnings	Other	Gross	Code	Absence	Earned	Balance

Deductions										Net Pay
Tax Sheltered Annuity	Federal Tax	State Tax	City Tax	Retirement	Medical Ins.	Credit Union	United Appeal			

Name		Check No.	Date	Total Amount	
					PLEASE DETACH AND RETAIN THIS STATEMENT. It is a record of earnings and deductions as reported to the federal and state governments.

Student Payroll Records

Many libraries handle student wages separately from the regular payroll. In the past, student wage rates were often below the national minimum wage and many payroll clerks kept student payroll records separated from those of other employee classifications in order to prevent confusion over different wage rates. In other instances, students may be scheduled on a different payroll period to avoid impact on the payroll office workload. Finally, as the federal government becomes more involved with grants, loans, and wage supplements (work-study programs, for example), there is an additional reason to keep student payroll records segregated.

When it comes to the mechanics of recording student hours, the same recordkeeping rules apply. Hours may be recorded by a time clock or entered manually on a time sheet by the student. In either case, each record should be signed by the student, attesting to the accuracy of the hours claimed, and each card must bear the signature of the student's supervisor, who certifies that the student's claim is valid and that the hours submitted are approved for payment (see figure 43).

General Comments and Suggestions

In instances where the library generates the payroll, the actual preparation of checks from basic payroll records (time sheets and/or time cards) may be accomplished in a variety of ways, including the use of automated check preparation equipment. Whether or not the payroll deductions are programmed to be handled automatically or are dealt with manually, the system must be designed to meet the requirements of regulatory agencies outside the library as well as the library itself.

Here are some suggestions to keep in mind if you include payroll recordkeeping in your internal accounting system.

1. Make certain your account clerk has an up-to-date list of all employees who are represented by payroll records.

2. Keep your supervisors and employees informed about all payroll regulations which affect them.

3. With your account clerk, prepare a payroll policy and procedure manual and provide means by which it can be updated as changes occur.

4. Identify a backup for the account clerk—someone who knows how to handle the payroll routines in the absence of the account clerk. It is usually possible to postpone a report or put off paying invoices for a day or two, *but payroll and paychecks will not wait.*

FIGURE 43. Record of hours worked by a student.

Left card (Miami University Student Time Card):

335
LIBRARY WG

Miami University Student Time Card

PERIOD ENDING 1/9/81

RATE 3.10

VALID FOR THIS DEPARTMENT ONLY

NO. OF MEALS

BR
LU
DR

CODES - FOR OFFICE USE ONLY

| 2 | 4 | 00 | 9 | 34 | | | 152 |
| 2 | 4 | 00 | 9 | | | | 152 |

FOR ACCOUNTING USE ONLY

REGULAR — O.T. — MEALS

0200032120152

VALID FOR THIS STUDENT ONLY

1
2 *Shipping*
   DEPARTMENT
3
4
5 *Mail clerk*
6 TYPE OF WORK PERFORMED
7 WORK HAS BEEN PERFORMED IN A SATISFACTORY MANNER.
8 APPROVED _____
9 DEPARTMENT HEAD OR DIRECTOR

1 2 3 4 5 6 7 8 9 10 11 12 13 14 15 16 17 18 19 20 21 22 23 24 25 26 27 28 29 30 31 32 33 34 35 36 37 38 39 40 41 42 43 44 45 46 47 48 49 50 51 52 53 54 55 56 57 58 59 60 61 62 63 64 65 66 67 68 69 70 71 72 73 74 75 76 77 78 79 80

Right card:

1ST WEEK		3RD WEEK	
DATE	HRS. WORKED	DATE	HRS. WORKED
SAT		SAT	
SUN		SUN	
12/15 MON	1½	MON	
12/16 TUE	3	TUE	
12/17 WED	3½	WED	
12/18 THU	4	THU	
12/19 FRI	0	FRI	
SUB TOTAL	12	SUB TOTAL	0

DO NOT FOLD SPINDLE OR MUTILATE THIS CARD

2ND WEEK		4TH WEEK	
DATE	HRS. WORKED	DATE	HRS. WORKED
SAT		SAT	
SUN		SUN	
MON		MON	
TUE		TUE	
WED		WED	
THU		THU	
FRI		FRI	
SUB TOTAL	0	SUB TOTAL	0

12

GRAND TOTAL HOURS

I UNDERSTAND THAT FOR ALL EMPLOYMENT AT MIAMI UNIVERSITY I AM NOT TO WORK MORE THAN A TOTAL OF 40 HOURS IN ANY ONE WORK WEEK AND AGREE TO ABIDE BY OTHER LIMITATIONS IMPOSED BY CWSP.

STUDENT SIGNATURE

Jennifer Canyon

IMMEDIATE SUPERVISOR

Chapter 5.
Describing Your System: Statistics, Reports, Audits, and Systems Maintenance

REPORTS FOR DECISIONS

A large percentage of the benefits to be derived from your internal accounting system come from the reports it provides. Management needs to know how and at what rate the budget is being spent, the status of the free balance, and what obligations are still to be paid. If you are spending large amounts of money rapidly, you can't wait for a monthly computer printout from a central administrative unit to tell you where you stand financially. That's one of the basic reasons for your manual internal accounting system: something that is simple, responsive, easily controlled, and that can provide you with up-to-the-minute accurate data when you need it. When management has reliable fiscal data available, it is easier to make prudent decisions.

By setting up your recordkeeping with the capacity to produce daily balances in every account, you guarantee the availability of current information. It is unlikely that you'll ever need to provide daily balances on a regular basis, but when necessary, such as near the end of a fiscal period, you should have the ability to do so.

Simplified Reporting

The use of flexible, preprinted report forms allows you to issue reports as many times a month as needed. If library collection development staff need closer monitoring of funds, this report may be issued weekly. You can quickly transfer figures from your account ledger with the fill-in-the-blank format of the forms. Such reports can be especially helpful management tools as spending deadlines approach.

In those instances where more frequent reporting is required, verbal reports are possible. However, they should be made only by the person who supervises or is ultimately responsible for the internal accounting system, not by the clerk who keeps the records. Giving out information verbally can lead to serious misunderstandings. Therefore, if you choose that method, make sure it is done by someone who is paid to take the responsibility for any errors that occur.

Giving out too much information can be wasteful, especially when that information is directed to those who don't need it for decision making. If you set up your report distribution on a need-to-know basis, you will restrict reports to a small, manageable list of knowledgeable people whose jobs require the information that you are providing.

Budget Reports

Budget reports (see figure 44) are usually issued primarily to administrators. Their purpose is to indicate the status of official budget allocations. Comparing one set of these reports to another previously issued set indicates the level of activity and the spending patterns for the various allocations. These reports should state the allocation for each fund group, the encumbrance and expenditure totals if needed, and the free balance. It may also be helpful to show the percentage of monies committed, which provides an indication of how much of the total allocation has been committed.

Often, more detailed budget reports are required. The extent of the detail provided varies from library to library; no single format will serve all. Such reports may be issued semiannually or quarterly. However,

FIGURE 44. Library budget report example.

Budget Report

Period Covered _____   Date _____

Account	Allocation	Encumbrance	Expenditure	Balance	% of Funds Committed
Books					
Standing Orders					
Approval Plans					
Periodicals					
Totals					
Operating Expenses					
Supplies					
Equipment					
Contractual					
Telephone					
Postage					
Miscellaneous					
Interlibrary Loan					
Binding					
Travel					
Totals					

copies to: (Director)   (Assistant Directors)   (Acquisitions Librarian)   (Serials Librarian)

monthly reports, if examined for trends and potential budget problems, are more meaningful to those responsible for the budget than less frequently issued reports.

Figure 45 and 46 present more examples of types of budget reports you can adapt to your own situation. We have included an example of a budget planning form.

FIGURE 45. Example of form to be issued after last working day of each month.

Monthly Financial Statement
Library Name

Period Covered _____

Allocation Code	Account Description	Allocation	Committed This Month	Committed to Date	Free Balance
115	Books	$	$	$	$
116	Periodicals				
117	Media				
118	Continuations				
119	Miscellaneous				
120	Supplies				
121	Equipment & Furniture				
122	Maintenance Agreements				
123	Equipment Leasing				
124	Automation Services				
125	Postage				
126	Travel				
	TOTAL	$	$	$	$

cc: Board Members
Director
Assistant Director
Acquisitions Librarian
Serials Librarian

FIGURE 46. Example of budget-planning form.

Budget Planning Summary
Library Name

Department _____

Expenditure Area	1979 Actual Expenditure	1980 Actual Expenditure	1981 Original Appropriation	1981 Actual Expenditure	1981 Budget Request	1982 Actual Appropriation
Wages and Salaries						
Fringe Benefits						
TOTAL Personnel Costs						
Library Materials						
New Equipment Purchases						
Other Operating Costs						
TOTAL Other Than Personnel						
TOTAL OPERATING COSTS						
Overhead Charges (utilities, etc.)						
NET OPERATING COSTS						
Interest Charges						
Construction Funds						
TOTAL COSTS						

Subaccount Reports for Book and Periodical Funds

While the budget reports serve as a means of explaining activity in the total library allocation, and especially for operating funds, more detailed subaccount reports may be required by the library administration and the book selectors.

These subaccount reports are issued in order to keep the selectors abreast of the status of their funds as encumbrances and expenditures are recorded, discounts credited, and additional charges deducted. The administration needs to be aware of which funds are being expended with regularity and which funds appear to have surplus monies. The acquisitions librarian needs such subaccount information before placing additional orders.

Guidelines

These subaccount reports should be issued once a month, and more often if feasible. Someone should be identified as the person to contact for verbal fund balances issued between written reports. Ideally, this person should be aware of any backlog in preparing purchase orders and able to indicate approximately how many requests are awaiting processing. Guidelines should also be established indicating who is allowed to have fund balance information on demand. For example, in an academic situation you may find it best to restrict specific fund balances to librarians and refer the faculty to an appropriate librarian for information.

The subaccount reports should include the fund name and/or code, the allocation, and the free balance remaining to be spent. Total encumbrances to date and total expenditures to date may also be included. However, inclusion of the last 2 figures is usually meaningless to the selectors and may create needless worry on their part if they attempt to determine why there are more encumbrances than expenditures or vice versa. The selectors should be concerned only with the allocations for their funds and with the balances remaining. Their goal should be to reduce the free balance to zero by the announced spending deadline.

Examples

Figures 47 and 48 present examples of academic subaccount reports for books and periodicals. Figure 47 also includes a percent committed column. The report cover page would include the date, the recipient, who to contact in case of questions, and any additional perti-

nent information. This first example is for a library organized by divisions and with many subject funds. Another part of this same subaccount report is for the library's designated funds—that is, those funds earmarked for reference areas, replacement purchases, periodicals, and any additional library funds for internal materials purchases. Figure 48 is for a library listing its funds alphabetically.

Public library subaccounts may be arranged by branch or by types of materials (see figure 49). The reports may appear less complex than academic library reports, which often include many subject funds.

Follow-up Questions

When subaccount reports are released, a question sure to arise from at least one selector is: "Why do I have more money now than was indicated in the last report?" "Why am I broke now when I had $300.00 on the previous report? I have not sent in any new orders." This situation occurs because discounts are credited back to the subaccounts. Also, funds may seem to disappear overnight when received materials cost more than encumbered.

STATISTICS IN THE MANUAL SYSTEM

Many statistics—for example, the average cost of a book purchased in a specific subject category—can be gleaned from a manual system, but it is a laborious, expensive job. The task may become so time-consuming, in fact, that unless the statistics required cannot be gotten easily from some other source, attempting to retrieve them from the internal accounting system should be considered only as a last resort. Unlike automated accounting systems, which can be programmed to provide a variety of statistics as a system by-product, most manual systems do not lend themselves to the gathering of statistics without a great deal of effort. If your internal accounting staff is required to spend full time posting records and compiling reports, then gathering statistics will require overtime or else the regular, daily work will suffer.

If the system must produce a minimum of statistics, design your recordkeeping to produce daily, weekly, and monthly balances which can be quickly compiled and presented in a simple format. This "simple format" can easily be nothing more than the old standby: the printed form. Your account clerk needs only to fill in the blanks, add a date, and photocopy as

FIGURE 47. A library organized by divisions, with many subject fund subaccounts.

Sciences			
Department	Allocations	Balance Free to Spend	% Committed
01 Aeronautics			
03 Botany			
04 Chemistry			
10 Geology			
13 Mathematics and Statistics			
14 Microbiology			
17 Physics			
24 Zoology			
33 Home Economics			
45 Engineering Technology			
46 Pulp and Paper Technology			
48 Systems Analysis			
58 Nursing			
59 Maps			
65 Institute of Environmental Sciences			
SCIENCE TOTAL			

% Committed _____

Humanities			
05 Classics			
07 English			
08 French & Italian			
11 German, Russian, & East Asian Languages			
16 Philosophy			
19 Psychology			
20 Religion			
22 Spanish & Portuguese			
23 Communications & Theatre			
35 Educational Media			
42 Architecture			
43 Art			
44 Music			
HUMANITIES TOTAL			

% Committed _____

FIGURE 47. A library organized by divisions, with many subject funds subaccounts (continued).

Social Sciences			
Department	Allocations	Balance Free to Spend	% Committed
02 Aerospace Studies			
09 Geography			
12 History			
15 Naval Science			
18 Political Science			
21 Sociology & Anthropology			
25 Educational Leadership			
26 Educational Psychology			
27 Personnel & Guidance			
29 Teacher Education			
31 HPE			
34 Industrial Education			
36 Accountancy			
37 Business Analysis			
38 Economics			
39 Finance			
40 Management			
41 Marketing Management			
47 Office Administration			
SOCIAL SCIENCE TOTAL			

% Committed ———

Library Designated Funds			
06 Humanities Book Replacements			
30 Social Science Book Replacements			
49 Documents			
50 Social Sciences Reference			
51 Humanities Reference			
52 Sciences Reference			
53 Sciences Book Replacements			
56 Director's Fund			
57 Technical Processing			
60 Periodicals			
60A Sciences			
60B Social Sciences			
60C Humanities			
60H Replacements			
66 Instructional Materials			
67 Children's Literature			
72 Fiction			
79 Standing Orders			
80 Record Library			
99 Approval Plan			
TOTAL DESIGNATED FUNDS			

% Committed ———

FIGURE 48. A library listing subaccount funds alphabetically.

Book Budget FY 80					
Date _____ Period covered _____					
Department	Allocation	Encumbered	Spent	Total	Free Balance
03 Art					
07 Botany					
08 Business					
11 Chemistry					
13 Economics					
15 Education					
17 English					
18 Foreign Language					
31 Geography/Geology					
35 History					
37 Home Economics					
40 Journalism					
43 Mathematics					
46 Music					
47 Philosophy					
49 Physical Education					
55 Physics					
59 Political Science					
61 Psychology					
65 Sociology/Anthropology					
66 Speech					
67 Speech Pathology					
68 Technology					
69 Theatre Arts					
70 Zoology					
80 Discretionary Fund					
TOTALS					

FIGURE 49. Public library subaccounts.

	Allocation	Free Balance
Library Name		
Date of Report _____	Period Covered _____	
Branch A		
Adult	_____	_____
Juvenile	_____	_____
Branch B		
Adult	_____	_____
Juvenile	_____	_____
Branch C		
Adult	_____	_____
Juvenile	_____	_____
Totals	_____	_____

many copies as necessary to satisfy your distribution list. It may not win any prizes for layout, design, and printing, but it will serve the purpose. Since much of the information it provides will be out-of-date in a few days, the report may be discarded as soon as an updated version arrives to replace it.

Gathering statistics from your manual system in any other way will be expensive and time-consuming. You may be able to handle a one-time request, but if you're asked to provide a set of statistics again and again, either find a way to build that capability into the basic recordkeeping routines or dispense with the request altogether.

If you are tempted to explore gathering statistics on a grand scale, talk with some of your vendors before you push your manual system and your staff beyond their limits. Many larger library vendors for both books and periodicals have highly automated systems; some offer management reports which provide records of detailed activity in their customer accounts. Why attempt for yourself what you may have only to ask your vendor to do for you? Some of the reports are free and others are available for a minimum charge. You should discuss your report needs with your area customer representatives and determine what your vendors can do for you. At first glance an annual charge for some management reports may seen unnecessarily expensive, but that report series could eliminate the need for another clerical position to furnish the same information.

AUDITS

Auditors are much maligned and misunderstood. They have an unnatural interest in finding out how you handle or mishandle your accounting routines. They worry about your checks and balances, your fiscal controls, and the degree of consistency with which your system operates.

Audits cover everything the library purchases: all goods and services. An auditor may check to make certain that employees whose names are on the payroll are actually on the job and are working the hours being claimed on the time card. Because employees have been known to turn in payroll records for hours worked when they were not physically present on the job (such as during holiday periods), an auditor monitors this area through periodic checks. Equipment and furniture also fall under the auditor's scrutiny. They not only need to be identified and placed in an office inventory, but also must be identified frequently in spot inventories to ascertain that they are still physically part of the capital equipment.

The audit trail is a logical sequence of filed purchasing and accounting documents with which you have identified the steps from purchase to payment. It must be clearly obvious and readily available. Establishing good audit trails will make performance audits a pleasant experience for both the library and the auditor. According to Eric L. Kohler's *A Dictionary for Accountants:* ''A 'good' audit trail is one where the labor of tracing transactions to original documents has been reduced to a minimum; such trails are essential, built-in features of *systems of accounts*'' (p. 47).

There are considerable benefits to be realized from a thorough audit. Whether your organization requires an audit or not, you can learn a great deal about your accounting system when an auditor takes an unbiased look at it. An auditor who is willing to share his/her findings with you will be able to do more than point out the problem areas. S/he can offer suggestions for improvements, suggestions which might not have occured to you and your staff. Having seen a variety of accounting systems, auditors can be a gold mine of information in terms of helpful hints and suggestions. When you find an auditor willing to help you with your accounting problems, take advantage of the offer. Your willingness to listen will identify you as one who is determined to use the most effective accounting routines, the kind of manager with whom every auditor enjoys working.

Types of Auditors

If there is no requirement for your system to be audited, you might suggest that arrangements be made for someone from your central accounting staff or an outside accounting firm to perform an informal audit. No, you are not asking for trouble by setting up an audit; you are merely arranging for an impartial appraisal from which you should be able to reap a rich reward in the form of suggestions for improvement. If you want to be on top of your system, making certain it is effective and efficient, here's one method for analysis that is difficult to beat.

There are at least 3 categories of auditors with whom you may expect to deal, depending upon the kind of library (public, academic, or special) in which you work: outside or external auditor, internal auditor, or governmental auditor.

The outside or external auditor is usually a representative of a consulting firm of accountants hired by and working independently of your library with a charge to examine your organization's financial condition and render an opinion.

The internal auditor is an employee of the library or parent organization. Operating independently within the organization, the internal auditor reviews the day-to-day accounting activities and advises the administrators of any deviations from the accepted accounting practices.

The government auditor is on the payroll of a governmental agency and, depending on the agency, audits his/her own agency, other government agencies, or organizations doing business with the government.

You might find yourself being audited by members of all 3 of these groups: an internal auditor who routinely examines library fine receipts, payroll time cards, or petty cash funds; an outside or independent firm of accounts who audit the organization's financial records and indirectly those of the library; and at least a couple of governmental auditors—one from another state agency (the state auditor's office), who regularly reviews the purchasing and accounting transactions of the organization and library, and a number of federal auditors who periodically audit the administration of federal grants and programs.

Types of Audits

Audits may be broken down into several categories. J. A. Cashin (*Handbook for Auditors,* pp. 1–11) identified 5 kinds of audits: (1) financial, (2) operational; (3) compliance; (4) performance; and (5) special reviews. In one way or another, all these may apply to libraries.

A financial audit is a review of the organization's financial records and accounting procedures by the auditor, who is responsible for determining whether or not those records, reports, and accounting procedures are accurate and reliable.

An operational audit is an audit of other operations which do not normally come under the auditor's jurisdiction, but which for any number of reasons require a special audit. An example might involve the suggestion made earlier in this chapter for calling in an auditor to evaluate the overall effectiveness of a unit which is not normally subject to audits.

A *compliance audit* involves an internal auditor reviewing the activity in a library governmental grant to make certain that the library is in full compliance with the governmental guidelines.

A *performance audit* is one of the most common audits. In most organizations it is a continuous process of auditing purchasing, receiving, and payment records to make certain that these transactions are carried out according to established guidelines and that proper fiscal controls are maintained as the organization's monies are spent. The performance audit may involve an internal auditor asking to see the order and payment records relating to several books s/he has identified from the card catalog. As s/he reviews the purchase order, receiving forms, and invoice and payment records, the auditor will be looking for accuracy, consistency, and compliance with the organization's purchasing and accounting policies.

A *special review* is an audit which does not fall under any of the other audit catagories. Since the other audits cover practically every aspect of any potential library audit, there is little left to fall under this heading, except perhaps the kind of special fact-finding review that is ordered when a library fiscal program has been found to be badly managed to the point of disaster or when any other emergency situations arise requiring immediate analysis for decision-making purposes. A sudden discovery that records have been falsified, reports doctored, or funds mismanaged would call for a special review or audit.

Problem Situations

There are helpful and conscientious auditors and, unfortunately, there are also the less-than-helpful, the ones who see little in their jobs beyond finding mistakes. The helpful auditor will examine your records with an eye toward helping you improve the accuracy and reliability of your systems. The good auditor knows the many pitfalls and problems we can be expected to encounter, and s/he can give valuable advice on how to avoid those pitfalls and problems long before you encounter them. S/he is positive, alert, and knowledgeable and should be listened to and appreciated. Use him/her as a resource. S/he can make your job easier. If you are open and aboveboard and treat him/her as a friendly advisor, you will benefit from the relationship.

The negative auditor, and there are a few, is the person whose Sherlock Holmes approach to auditing will not permit him/her to get beyond looking for errors. When the announcement "the auditor is here to check the books" takes on the connotation of a threat, there is likely to be very little value gained from the audit. Making a helpful auditor out of a negative one may seem to be a fruitless venture, but if you are willing to take the time and exercise your diplomatic skills, the potential benefits can be well worth the investment. There is no guaranteed formula for approaching such a conversion, but if you are willing to open your books to the auditor, ask his/her advice and treat him/her with respect, you may be favorably impressed with the results.

Trial Audit

Conducting your own audit by setting up a dress rehearsal for the real thing is a way to find out how your system will fare in an actual audit situation. Even if your system never receives an audit, there is no reason why you shouldn't conduct your own. If you think you have a reliable, accurate system, conducting your own audit will simply confirm your opinions. If you are doubtful about some aspect of your system, a good audit can identify the problems you need to address. Knowing where the weaknesses are is the first step; without an audit, it is sometimes impossible to isolate the real trouble spots.

How do you go about it? Here are some examples:

1. If your purchase orders are recorded in your ledger by number, select a couple of dozen purchase order numbers at random and, using those numbers, locate the copy of each original in your file. Don't delegate this chore to one of your assistants. Do it yourself. It is too easy for someone who deals with the files on a daily basis to fail to recognize an error or to discount a seemingly minor problem—one which you might determine to be highly significant.

2. When you have the original purchase orders in hand, check each one to see if it shows: (a) order date; (b) date received; (c) estimated price; and (d) actual price.

3. If you pay by check or generate payment with a voucher, locate the actual documents you used to authorize payment, checking to see if: (a) the purchase order matches the invoice; (b) the payment was properly approved for payment; and (c) a copy of the approved invoice is attached to the payment document or can be easily located.

4. In the process of making these simple investigations, you may turn up questionable practices: a

missing invoice, misfiled documents or other errors. With the evidence in hand, discuss the problem you have found with your staff and review your procedures with an eye to improving the reliability of your system. Let the staff know that your impromptu audits will become a routine part of your management style.

Positive Approach

Whenever the subject of audits arises, do your best to impress your staff with the value of such periodic reviews. Take a positive approach to the audit. Use it as a means of identifying little problems before they can become big ones. Enlist the support of the staff by letting them know that you are more interested in locating the problems and taking corrective action than in assigning blame and taking disciplinary action. Solicit their help and your audits will begin to pay off. When the staff learns that your self-audits are primarily designed to improve the system, they'll pitch in and cooperate.

With periodic self-audits and a staff accustomed to having their files and records reviewed, you'll be in excellent shape to receive an outside auditor.

Surprise Audits

One final suggestion: How do you approach a surprise audit, especially when you have not trained your staff to work with an auditor? Of course there is an element of indecision involved whenever you are obliged to stop what you are doing and open doors to someone who wants to see how your system works. You might be right in the middle of a system change or halfway through the resolution of a complicated problem which has necessitated many of your records to be out of their normal files. You'd rather the auditor come back at a more convenient time and you wonder if you should attempt to somehow prevent him/her from seeing the mess your shop is in at the moment.

Forget the subterfuge. It might work, on the one hand, but on the other hand, it might not. If you were discovered attempting to mislead the auditor . . . well, you can imagine the possibilities, ranging from general suspicion to a full-fledged investigation. Take the surprise visitor aside, briefly describe your situation, and ask him/her where s/he would like to start. The auditor will appreciate your candor. You've saved him/her from having to take time from his/her audit to try to find out what's going on and you may be the lucky recipient of some truly valuable suggestions for improving the performance of your system. Honesty is the best policy.

It's a great time saver, builds rapport, and often leads directly to solutions to the problems you were addressing.

VISITS BY THE CENTRAL ADMINISTRATION

If your system serves as a check against the reports furnished from a central accounting system, and if it supplies information to that central accounting system, you may find it necessary to explain some of your internal routines to the central accounting office staff, especially if you have recently inherited them or are contemplating changes such as automation which could affect the way the central accountants treat your data.

Orientations

If you want the central accounting staff to accept your ideas or if they ask to look at your procedures, arrange a visit. Let them see what you do and how it ties in with their routines. If you open the door to them and request their advice and assistance, they may respond positively. They may not know anything about library purchasing and accounting requirements but, if you take the time to plan for the visit and show them the way your organization functions, they will be in a good position to offer you assistance which can make your task easier.

For example, when a midwestern academic library was able to demonstrate a need for better control over coding errors generated by the central accounting department, the accounting department agreed to allow the library to code its own requisitions. The result: practically no coding errors once the library began to handle its own coding. Why? Because the central accounting clerks routinely dealt with thousands of requisitions each month; included among them were those from the library. Consequently, there were errors. With the library account clerk coding only library requisitions, limited to a few standard codes, coding errors were dramatically reduced. If the central accounting staff had not known anything about the organization of the library internal system, they would never have imagined that the library could handle its own coding effectively.

Communication

Establishing effective paths of communication between the library and the central accounting system is basic to an efficient operation. It takes a moderate amount of effort on the part of the library but, if handled carefully, can provide tremendous benefits.

In the section dealing with auditing, we have explored the "open-door" policy that paves the way for better communication and understanding between the library and the auditor. This technique applies equally to other divisions of the central administration. The purchasing department, for example, can offer the library numerous worthwhile suggestions if the key people in that department know what the library is trying to accomplish. With an open-door policy, you have the potential to take advantage of what amounts to free consulting while at the same time building sound business relationships with your central administration staff.

On the other side of the coin, library staff can profit from knowing about the accounting or purchasing department. Finding out why reports, requisitions, vouchers, and other documents must be submitted in a certain format, for example, can give meaning to routine clerical chores performed, but not understood, by the library staff. When groups who work in different locations but who need to cooperate in order to serve an institutional need are brought together, the resulting sharing of ideas can provide benefits for everyone involved.

FILING AND FILE MAINTENANCE

Filing is not one of the more interesting activities in an office operation. Consequently, it may be neglected or left as a last-minute chore. However, filing is a necessary part of any business office operation. If a piece of paper or fiscal document is left unfiled or is filed incorrectly, it may be irretrievable when needed. A set of filing rules to fit your organizational needs should be devised and then followed consistently.

Do not attempt to apply standard library filing rules to an office situation. Follow a set of rules which are easily learned and have been adapted to your office routines. Use common sense and convenience in choosing where to locate the files. Some may be kept near the books or periodicals ordering area, for example, while others may be located where supplies are ordered. Still others may be needed where payments are initiated.

Filing Alternatives

There are several ways to file the fiscal documents which support your library financial transactions. Consistency is the one important factor to keep in mind, regardless of the filing system you select.

1. Documents on which control numbers appear may be filed numerically, in ascending or descending order. These documents may be housed together in one file or may be divided into separate files by the account allocation against which the transaction took place.
2. Documents may be filed by date and may be arranged with the most recent transaction at the front of the file or in reverse order.
3. Documents may be arranged by vendor. This is the most complex filing method to set up and maintain, requiring many decisions in order to determine filing sequence. When filed by vendor, the documents also may be separated by type of allocation so that different letters of the alphabet are used for each account (for example, Books, Supplies, etc.).

Filing Rules

Specific rules must be followed in setting up and maintaining any alphabetical file. These rules and any local modifications should appear in written form for easy reference whenever filing decisions must be made. If possible, the same person should always do the filing in order to allow consistent interpretation of the filing rules.

For example, here are sample rules which could be followed in a filing system:

1. Documents should be filed by last name when the vendor name consists of a first and last name: "Bufford Allen Co." would be filed under "Allen."
2. Vendors with names beginning with the same letter would be filed alphabetically, letter by letter. For example:
   Random
   Rodeco
   Rutgers
3. Similarly, following the letter-by-letter rule, "Rand" would precede "Random"; "Rod" would precede "Rodeco"; and "Ruta" would precede "Rutgers."
4. Initials precede names in filing. "G. Marshall" would precede "Granville Marshall."
5. Libraries often acquire materials from university presses. Consequently, a decision must be made about how to file documents relating to those presses. In this instance, any filing rule adopted is acceptable as long as it is applied uniformly throughout

the files. For example, these names are filed in simple alphabetical order:

> Lousiana State University Press
> MIT Press
> New York University Press
> Rutgers University Press

Most filing questions arise with press names such as "University of Kentucky Press," "University of Texas Press," or "University of Miami Press." These can be filed in either of 2 ways. One of these is to list them under "University" with file order determined by the city or state name, as in the following examples:

> University of Kentucky Press
> University of Miami Press
> University of Texas Press

Such an arrangement leads, of course, to a large number of documents filed under "University of." Preferable, and more useful, is filing by state or city, thus scattering the presses named "University of" throughout the alphabetical sequence. For example, a file might include University of Kansas Press between KTO Press and Knopf.

Either method is acceptable. Again, consistent application of the rule is the important point to remember.

6. Departments within universities often issue publications; these can become another filing problem. If it was decided to file university press publications under University of _____, then the subdivisions of the university itself should also be filed under University of _____, as in these examples:

> University of Miami. Department of Geology
> University of Miami. Department of Physics
> University of Texas. Department of Geology

If the university presses are filed under place name, the subdivisions of the university should also be filed by place name. Under the letter K, for example, would be listed:

> University of Kansas. Department of Educational Technology
> University of Kansas. Department of English
> University of Kentucky. School of Fine Arts
> University of Kentucky. School of Library Science

Once your alphabetical arrangement is determined, you will want to arrange the documents within a vendor name group in chronological order or numerical order by control number.

Older Files

File maintenance does not end with consistent following of rules and up-to-date filing. Files must also be rearranged and shifted seasonally. Before the end of each fiscal year, files must be set up for the new year. Files for the previous year must be removed and retired, and some older files can be stored. (The number of years that fiscal records must be kept will be determined by the legal requirements of the auditing body reviewing your library.)

Prior-year records can be filed tightly in files more compact than those in which current year records are kept, since they will not be accessed as frequently. Copies of older records would also be kept close by for possible use. When new fiscal-year transactions begin to take place, all files should be ready to use. By this time you should have also prepared all ledgers to be ready to record new transactions.

TIPS, HINTS, SUGGESTIONS

Simplicity

"KISS: Keep it simple, stupid" is a phrase frequently used to alert the unwary planner to the virtues of brevity and simplicity. Never did that phrase have a better application than in the design of a library internal accounting system. In no time at all, the overzealous planner can create a complex system which is geared to deal with every aspect of your fiscal routines. It's wonderful to have all that detail at your fingertips, but at what price?

First you must determine what you want to accomplish and then find the least complicated, most effective way to go about getting it done. For example, you may need to issue a series of periodic reports which will be used for management decisions, but will not be preserved once the decision-making process is completed. Design those reports on a series of standard formats which can be photocopied, preprinted, or mimeographed. At report time the clerk merely has to fill in the blanks, make the necessary number of copies, and distribute them. If the clerk has legible handwriting, there is no need to type the figures.

Design your internal accounting system in such a way that each account or fund shows a free balance as of the date the last expenditure or encumbrance was posted. At report time, the clerical effort needed to go through the series of accounts, picking off the free balances and posting them to the preprinted report form, is minimal.

In an internal system based upon a computerized program, don't permit the program to become overly complicated simply because the computer can provide a wide range of additional reports and statistics. Stick to the basics. Request only what you need to get the job done. If you have to absorb the cost of your computer services, you'll soon learn how important it is to keep your system costs to a minimum. As your system grows and as you need to meet increased demands for records and reports, increase your computer time accordingly. A pay-as-you-go approach complements your determination to keep your system simple and uncomplicated.

To prevent overburdening your account clerk with an excess of marginally useful recordkeeping, put together a list of the primary objectives for your system: something very simple and basic against which you will weight every decision affecting the scope and purpose of your system. Keep thise points in mind as you establish your guidelines:

1. Are the reports required by law—federal, state, local, or institutional?
2. Does this routine duplicate something already provided by someone else?
3. Does the service you intend to provide answer a real need? Does a manager need it in order to support or enhance a decision?
4. Can the service be provided cheaply with a minimum of clerical effort? Are the facts readily available?
5. Is there a cheaper, more direct way to compile reports and present the information?
6. What is the minimum service you can provide and still get the job done? Every additional cost you incur

increases the overall cost of your system, so keep the planning geared to the basics only.

Currency

If your internal records are to be of any value to you and your library, they must be current. The staff doing the bookkeeping must understand the importance of being up-to-date. Guidelines may be needed to ensure currency.

1. As soon as any kind of orders have been prepared, funds should be encumbered and the orders should be released for mailing, placed electronically, or phoned to the supplier. Encumbering must be handled expeditiously so that placing orders is not delayed. If encumbering is a lengthy, time-consuming task, it will become a target for complaints about delaying actual order initiation.
2. Similarly, as soon as materials are received and checked in, the invoices should be cleared for payment. If the library itself does not prepare the checks, there will be some delays while invoices and perhaps payment requisitions or vouchers are sent to another office. Nevertheless, if materials are checked in and invoices cleared expeditiously, some time will be saved.

Remember that delays in encumbering, expending, and in other financial transactions will subvert the purpose of your internal bookkeeping: a current, accurate, responsive financial system.

Bibliography

Aljian, George W. *Purchasing Handbook*. 3rd ed. New York: McGraw-Hill, 1973.

Baron, Harold and Steinfeld, Solomon C. *Practical Recordkeeping. Course I*. 4th ed. Cincinnati, OH: South-Western Publishing Co., 1975.

Cashin, James A. *Handbook for Auditors*. New York: McGraw-Hill, 1971.

Doyle, Dennis M. *Efficient Accounting and Recordkeeping*. New York: John Wiley, 1978.

Hoffman, H. H. *Simple Library Bookkeeping*. Rev. ed. Newport Beach, CA: Headway Publications, 1977.

Kohler, Eric L. *A Dictionary for Accountants*. 5th ed. Englewood Cliffs, NJ: Prentice-Hall, 1975.

Nygren, William V. *Business Forms Management*. New York: Amacon, 1980.

Sheff, Alexander L. *Bookkeeping Made Easy, with a Section on Business Mathematics*. New York: Barnes and Noble, 1966.

Glossary

Account Number. A number assigned to designate a specific account in a series of accounts.

Actual Cost. The final cost of a product or service, taking into account any additional or extra charges as well as any discounts. The actual price paid as opposed to the list price advertised.

Audit Trial. The route by which accounting transactions may be traced to original documents. As accounting documents (purchase requisitions or vouchers, invoices, and statements) are processed, the records maintained at each stage in the process comprise an audit trail.

Balance. The difference between expenditures and the allocation in an account or fund.

Balancing, The process of agreement. The figures *balance* or agree with a predetermined figure, or credits balance the expenditures.

Blanket Encumbrance. An encumbrance or commitment which covers a large number of goods or services, often without specifying each in detail beyond a total amount of money committed.

Business Manager. The person responsible for carrying out the business and financial affairs (purchasing, accounting, maintenance, and personnel) of the library.

Cash Flow. The process of tracing the organization's income and expenditures from the time funds are deposited until they are expended.

Clerk Treasurer. A title often given to public library administrators charged with budget preparation and disbursement, purchasing, and other business responsibilities.

Encumber. To commit, set aside, or earmark funds for a specific purpose in order to hold them in reserve until they can be formally expended.

Encumbrance. A commitment to pay at a future time. An amount of money set aside for a specific purpose.

Expend. To pay for goods or services. The actual process of paying.

Free Balance. After the balance between credits and expenditures is determined, the free balance is that amount which remains to be spent or committed; an unencumbered amount remaining in an account or fund.

Interest. The price paid for borrowing money, usually computed as a percent of the total amount borrowed.

Investments. For the purposes of this book, money put out to earn income. Some libraries may invest surplus funds with banks in order to earn money.

Invoice. A purchase document which describes the goods or services ordered and includes price, quantity, delivery, and any other limitations or conditions pertinent to the sale.

Job Description. A written description of the duties and responsibilities of a position in an organization. It may be written by the employee occupying the position, by management, or by a combination of both.

Log. A written chronological record of events or activities.

Multiple Order Form. A printed purchase order form printed and prepared in multiple copies. Often referred to as "multiple."

Object Codes or Standard Object Codes. The code number assigned to a particular "object" (that is, goods or services representing expenditures) for accounting and auditing purposes.

Operating Funds. Those funds designated for the purpose of conducting business.

Petty Cash. Cash kept on hand to pay for incidental expenses. Usually a small amount of money.

Pool Fund. Monies allocated to one fund to be expended for a variety of purposes. Purchasing all the library's books from a single "pool" fund rather than reallocating the money into a series of individual funds is an example.

Posting. Entering accounting data into a predetermined format, as in posting accounts on a ledger. Posting may be done manually or electronically.

Purchase Order. A formal commitment to purchase goods or services at a stated price. When accepted by the seller, the purchase order has the effect of a contract. The traditional 3″×5″ library book order form is an example of a purchase order.

Purchasing Agent. The person responsible for purchasing goods and services and for entering into formal contractual agreements. The acquisitions librarian may serve as the library "purchasing agent."

Refund. Money expended for goods and services and returned to the buyer by the seller for nondelivery of goods or a similar reason.

Requisition. A written request made by one department within an organization to another department in the same organization. The requisition may be prepared for goods or services or even funds.

Sheet Invoice. An invoice listing more than one item. For example, 50 individual book titles could be included on a single "sheet" invoice.

Statement. A document attesting to the status of an account or accounts. It is rendered by a vendor and lists recent transactions with the library customer.

Tax Exemption Number. A number provided by the Internal Revenue Service to an organization not subject to the payment of taxes. Vendors may request tax exemption numbers from qualifying libraries to document failure to collect specific taxes.

Temporary Purchase Order Number. A number temporarily assigned to implement telephone purchases or rush orders, usually limited to specific amounts and vendors. It is a convenient procedure adopted by many larger libraries.

Voucher. An accounting document which shows authority to make an expenditure. Voucher and requisition are often used interchangeably.

Supplies and Equipment: Selected Sources

This is not an exhaustive list. You should also check for local suppliers of these products.

Calculators:

Canon Business Machines, Inc.
3191 Red Hill Ave.
Costa Mesa, CA 92626

Monroe, The Calculator Co.
The American Rd.
Morris Plains, NJ 07950

Olivetti Corp. of America
155 White Plains Rd.
Tarrytown, NY 10591

Victor Comptometer Corp.
3900 North Rockwell St.
Chicago, IL 60618

Cash Registers:

Fidelity Products Co.
703 S. Pennsylvania Ave.
Minneapolis, MN 55426

Indiana Cash Drawer Co.
P.O. Box 236
Shelbyville, IN 46176

M-S Corp.
10711 Flower St.
Stanton, CA 90680

NCR Corp.
1700 S. Patterson Blvd.
Dayton, OH 45479

Victor Comptometer Corp.
3900 N. Rockwell St.
Chicago, IL 60618

Cash and Coin Sorters:

Fordham Equipment
3308 Edson Ave.
Bronx, NY 10469

National Stationers
2066–76 W. Hunting Park Ave.
Philadelphia, PA 19140

Check Machines (Writers and Signers):

Burroughs Corp.
Office Products Group
1150 University Ave.
Rochester, NY 14607

Cummins-Allison Corp.
4740 N. Ravinswood
Chicago, IL 60640

Forms, Accounting and Business:

Baker-Goodyear Co.
68 Boston Post Rd.
Branford, CT 06405

Moore Business Forms Inc.
1205 North Milwaukee Ave.
Glenview, IL 60025

NCR Corp.
1700 South Patterson Blvd.
Dayton, OH 45479

National Blank Book Co., Inc.
Holyoke, MA 01040

Standard Register
P.O. Box 1167
Dayton, OH 45401

UARCO, Inc.
Barrington, IL 60010

Ledgers:

> Georgia Pacific Corp.
> National Cover Div.
> 3810 Paule Ave.
> St. Louis, MO 63125

Ledgers, Card Systems:

> Acme Visible Records, Inc.
> 8900 W. Allview Dr.
> Crozet, VA 22932

> Shaw Walker Co.
> 1950 Townsend St.
> Muskegon, MI 49443

> Sperry Remington
> Box 1000
> Blue Bell, PA 19422

Library Suppliers:

> Brodart, Inc.
> 1609 Memorial Ave.
> Williamsport, PA 17705

> Demco Education Group
> Box 7488
> 2120 Fordem Ave.
> Madison, WI 53707

> Gaylord Bros., Inc.
> Box 4901
> Syracuse, NY 13221

> Highsmith Co., Inc.
> P.O. Box 25
> Fort Atkinson, WI 53538

Safes and Storage Boxes:

> Diebold, Inc.
> 818 Mulberry Rd., S.E.
> Canton, OH 44711

> Mosler Safe Co.
> 1561 Grand Blvd.
> Hamilton, OH 45012

Stamps (Dating, Numbering, Signatures, etc.):

> Hathaway Stamp Co.
> 627 Main
> Cincinnati, OH 45202

> Rubber Stamps, Inc.
> 16 W. 22nd St.
> New York, NY 10010

Time Cards:

> Cincinnati Time Recorder Co.
> 1749 Central Ave.
> Cincinnati, OH 45214

> Clocks, Inc.
> 2445 N. Freeway
> Houston, TX 77009

> Lathem Time Recorder
> 140 Selig Dr., S.W.
> Atlanta, GA 30336

> National Time and Signal Corp.
> 21802 Wyoming Ave.
> Oak Park, MI 48237

Index
Compiled by Linda Schexnaydre